CONTEMPORARY'S

GED

MATHEMATICS EXERCISE BOOK

Jerry Howett

Mc Graw Hill **Wright Group**

Executive Editor: Linda Kwil
Creative Director: Michael E. Kelly
Marketing Manager: Sean Klunder
Production Manager: Genevieve Kelley

Interior Design by Think Design Group LLC

Wright Group

Printed in the United States of America.

Send all inquiries to:
Wright Group/McGraw-Hill
130 E. Randolph, Suite 400
Chicago, IL 60681

ISBN 0-8092-2237-X

9 10 11 12 QDP 09 08

Table of Contents

Introduction

This exercise book offers practice problems to help you prepare for the GED Mathematics Test. The eleven main sections correspond to the chapters in Contemporary's *GED Mathematics*.

The **Pretest** will help you decide which sections you need to concentrate on. After the Pretest, there is instruction on using the Casio *fx*-260 calculator, the only calculator permitted on the GED Test. You will also find instruction on filling in a number grid and a coordinate plane grid.

Each main section of the book is divided into three parts.

The first part is called **Basic Skills**. Here you will review vocabulary, computation, and estimation. Remember that mathematical skills are cumulative. The skills you master with whole numbers, decimals, and fractions will be applied in later sections. Be sure that you can solve all the problems in Basic Skills before you go on.

The next part of each section is called **GED Practice, Part I**. Here you will find multiple-choice problems that permit the use of a calculator. You will also practice writing your answers on a number grid.

The last part of each section, **GED Practice, Part II**, has more multiple-choice problems to be solved without the use of a calculator. You will practice further with number grids and coordinate plane grids.

Complete solutions and explanations are in the **Answer Key**.

Finally, a full-length **Practice Test** will help you decide whether you are ready to take the GED Mathematics Test.

The GED Mathematics Test

The GED Mathematics Test consists of two parts, each with 25 problems and each with a time limit of 45 minutes. Part I allows you to work the problems with a calculator; Part II does not. Both parts of the test include word problems with five multiple-choice answers as well as problems you must solve before recording the answer on a number grid or on a coordinate plane grid.

Content areas covered on the Test include

- Number Sense and Operations (20–30%)
- Data Analysis, Statistics, and Probability (20–30%)
- Measurement and Geometry (20–30%)
- Algebra (20–30%)

Mathematical abilities tested are

- Procedural (15–25%)
- Conceptual (25–35%)
- Problem Solving (50%)

Mathematics

Directions: This Pretest will help you evaluate your strengths and weaknesses in mathematics. The test is in three parts. Part 1 includes number operations (arithmetic) as well as data analysis, probability, and statistics. Part 2 tests measurement and geometry, and Part 3 tests algebra. You may use the formulas on page 130 during the test.

Solve every problem that you can. When you finish, check the answers with the Answer Key on page 10. Then look at the Evaluation Chart on page 13. Use the chart as a guide to tell you the areas in which you need the most work.

Pretest Answer Grid, Part 1

1 _____

2 _____

3 _____

4 _____

5 _____

6 _____

7 _____

8 _____

9 _____

10 _____

11 _____

12 _____

13 ① ② ③ ④ ⑤   25 ① ② ③ ④ ⑤

14 ① ② ③ ④ ⑤   26 ① ② ③ ④ ⑤

15 ① ② ③ ④ ⑤   27 ① ② ③ ④ ⑤

16 ① ② ③ ④ ⑤   28 ① ② ③ ④ ⑤

17 ① ② ③ ④ ⑤   29 ① ② ③ ④ ⑤

18 ① ② ③ ④ ⑤   30 ① ② ③ ④ ⑤

19 ① ② ③ ④ ⑤

20 ① ② ③ ④ ⑤

21 ① ② ③ ④ ⑤

22 ① ② ③ ④ ⑤

23 ① ② ③ ④ ⑤

24 ① ② ③ ④ ⑤

PRETEST

Part 1

Number Operations, Data Analysis, Statistics, and Probability

Directions: Solve each problem.

1. For the numbers 683 and 2329, round each number to the nearest hundred. Then find the product of the rounded numbers.

2. Round 46.3795 to the nearest hundredth.

3. $10\frac{1}{3}$ is how much more than $7\frac{8}{9}$?

4. Find 40% of 65.

5. 21 is what percent of 28?

6. Find the interest on $4000 at 3.5% annual interest for 1 year 6 months.

7. Sanford bought two shirts for $24.95 each and a pair of pants for $39.95. He paid with a $100 bill. Assuming he paid no sales tax, how much change did he receive?

8. Maureen drove for 1.5 hours at an average speed of 62 mph and then for another half hour at an average speed of 24 mph. How far did she drive altogether?

9. What is the value of 120^2?

10. The budget for Milltown was $3.55 million in 1990. In 1995 the budget was $4.15 million, and in 2000 the budget was $5.3 million. By how much did the budget increase from 1995 to 2000?

11. Express the ratio of 56 to 84 in simplest form.

12. For every $2 that Tom saves, he spends $18. Write the ratio of the amount Tom spends to the amount Tom makes.

Choose the correct answer to each problem.

13. In the number 18,465,000, what is the value of the digit 4?

    (1)   400
    (2)   4,000
    (3)   40,000
    (4)   400,000
    (5)   4,000,000

14. Which of the following is the approximate quotient of $5658 \div 82$?

    (1)   7
    (2)   70
    (3)   140
    (4)   700
    (5)   1400

15. Which of the following is the same as $8(9 + 2)$?

    (1) $8 \times 9 + 8$
    (2) $8 \times 9 + 2$
    (3) $8 \times 9 + 8 \times 2$
    (4) $9(8 + 2)$
    (5) $2(8 + 9)$

16. Arlette makes $2467 each month. Which expression represents her yearly income?

    (1) 4($2467)

    (2) 12($2467)

    (3) $\frac{\$2467}{12}$

    (4) $\frac{\$2467}{4}$

    (5) $\frac{12}{\$2467}$

17. Tom wants to strip and repaint all 16 windows in his house. So far he has refinished 12 of the windows. Which of the following does *not* represent the part of the entire job that he has completed?

    (1) 0.75

    (2) $\frac{3}{4}$

    (3) $\frac{12}{100}$

    (4) 75%

    (5) $\frac{12}{16}$

18. Michiko drove 364 miles in $7\frac{1}{2}$ hours. Which expression represents her average driving speed in miles per hour?

    (1) 7.5(364)

    (2) $\frac{7.5}{364}$

    (3) 2(364 + 7.5)

    (4) $\frac{364 + 7.5}{2}$

    (5) $\frac{364}{7.5}$

19. The answer to $\sqrt{5184}$ is between which of the following pairs of numbers?

    (1) 40 and 50
    (2) 50 and 60
    (3) 60 and 70
    (4) 70 and 80
    (5) 80 and 90

20. On Friday 235 people attended a performance at the Community Playhouse. On Saturday 260 people attended the performance. Everyone paid $12 for a ticket. Which expression represents the total receipts, in dollars, for the two performances?

    (1) $\frac{235 + 260}{12}$

    (2) 12(235 + 260)

    (3) 12(235) + 260

    (4) 235 + 12(260)

    (5) 12 × 235 × 260

21. The Simpsons paid $212.95 for 100 gallons of heating oil. To the nearest cent, what was the price per gallon of the heating oil?

    (1) $2.95
    (2) $2.19
    (3) $2.15
    (4) $2.13
    (5) $2.10

22. Which expression is equal to the product of $\frac{1}{3}$ and $2\frac{1}{4}$?

    (1) $\frac{1}{3} \times \frac{4}{9}$

    (2) $\frac{3}{1} \times \frac{4}{9}$

    (3) $\frac{1}{3} \times \frac{9}{4}$

    (4) $\frac{1}{3} \times \frac{1}{4}$

    (5) $\frac{3}{1} \times \frac{9}{4}$

23. Scientists estimate that the temperature at the core of the sun is 27,000,000°F. Which of the following represents the Fahrenheit temperature in scientific notation?

    (1) 2.7×10^4
    (2) 2.7×10^5
    (3) 2.7×10^6
    (4) 2.7×10^7
    (5) 2.7×10^8

24. From a 2-pound bag of flour, Marcella took $\frac{1}{4}$ pound to bake bread. Which expression tells the weight of the flour left in the bag?

    (1) $2 - 0.25$
    (2) $2 - 1.4$
    (3) $2 - 0.14$
    (4) $2 - 0.025$
    (5) $2.5 - 2$

Problems 25 and 26 refer to the following information.

For every dollar spent on summer youth programs in Milltown, 80 cents goes directly to program services. The rest of the budget is spent on staff salaries.

25. What is the ratio of the amount spent on staff salaries to the total budget for the youth programs?

    (1) 1:10
    (2) 1:8
    (3) 1:5
    (4) 1:4
    (5) 1:2

26. The budget for the summer soccer program in Milltown is $20,000. How much is spent on staff salaries?

    (1) $10,000
    (2) $ 8,000
    (3) $ 5,000
    (4) $ 4,000
    (5) $ 2,000

27. The table lists the selling prices of four houses on Elm Street. What is the mean selling price of the houses?

12 Elm Street	$ 93,000
17 Elm Street	$ 98,000
23 Elm Street	$105,000
36 Elm Street	$128,000

    (1) $ 93,000
    (2) $ 99,000
    (3) $103,500
    (4) $106,000
    (5) $128,000

28. A countywide Little League sold 2000 raffle tickets for a new car. Members of the Milltown Little League sold 125 of the raffle tickets. What is the probability that the winning ticket was sold by a member of the Milltown Little League?

(1) $\frac{1}{6}$

(2) $\frac{1}{8}$

(3) $\frac{1}{10}$

(4) $\frac{1}{12}$

(5) $\frac{1}{16}$

Problems 29 and 30 refer to the graph below.

SOURCES OF U.S.
WARMING GAS EMISSIONS

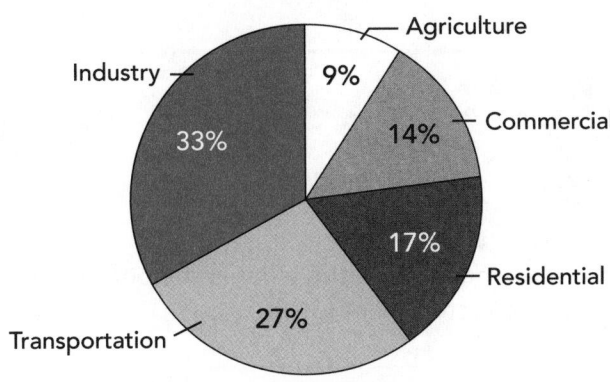

Source: Environmental Protection Agency

29. According to the graph, industry and transportation together produce what fraction of warming gas emissions?

(1) $\frac{1}{5}$

(2) $\frac{1}{4}$

(3) $\frac{2}{5}$

(4) $\frac{3}{5}$

(5) $\frac{3}{4}$

30. For every pound of warming gas produced by agriculture, how many pounds of warming gas are produced by transportation?

(1) 1.0
(2) 1.3
(3) 2.0
(4) 2.7
(5) 3.0

Answers are on page 10.

PRETEST

Pretest Answer Grid, Part 2

1 _____

2 _____

3 _____

4 _____

5 ① ② ③ ④ ⑤   11 ① ② ③ ④ ⑤

6 ① ② ③ ④ ⑤   12 ① ② ③ ④ ⑤

7 ① ② ③ ④ ⑤   13 ① ② ③ ④ ⑤

8 ① ② ③ ④ ⑤   14 ① ② ③ ④ ⑤

9 ① ② ③ ④ ⑤   15 ① ② ③ ④ ⑤

10 ① ② ③ ④ ⑤   16 ① ② ③ ④ ⑤

PART 2

Measurement and Geometry

Directions: Solve each problem.

1. A meeting room is 50 feet wide. What is the width of the room in yards?

2. Eight kilograms are equal to how many grams?

3. What is the length, in inches, of the line between points x and y on the ruler?

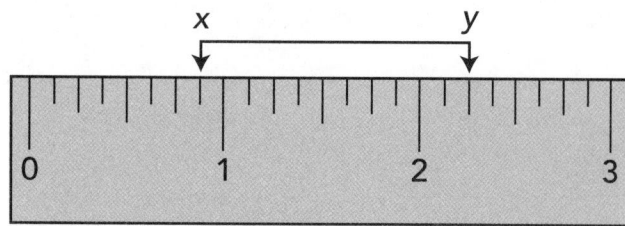

4. At an average driving speed of 60 mph, how far can Marta drive in 2 hours 15 minutes?

Choose the correct answer to each problem.

5. Which expression represents the length, in feet, of 6 bricks, each 9 inches long, laid end to end?

(1) $\frac{6 \times 12}{9}$

(2) $\frac{6 \times 9}{12}$

(3) $\frac{12}{6 \times 9}$

(4) $6 \times 9 \times 12$

(5) $12 + 6 \times 9$

6. To the nearest meter, what is the perimeter of the rectangle below?

(1) 6
(2) 7
(3) 9
(4) 11
(5) 12

2.1 m

3.5 m

7. What is the volume, in cubic inches, of a rectangular box that is 1 foot long, 8 inches wide, and 5 inches high?

(1) 80
(2) 120
(3) 240
(4) 360
(5) 480

PRETEST

8. Which expression represents the area of the shaded part of the figure below?

   (1) $\frac{23 \times 15}{2}$

   (2) $2(23) + 2(15)$

   (3) 23×15

   (4) $23^2 + 15^2$

   (5) $2(23 + 15)$

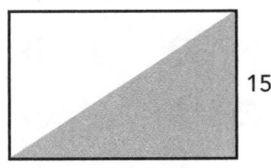

9. A circular reflecting pool has a radius of 10 meters. Rounded to the nearest 10 square meters, what is the surface area of the bottom of the pool?

   (1)　30
   (2)　60
   (3) 260
   (4) 310
   (5) 620

10. The measurement of $\angle x$ is 43.5°. Find the measure of $\angle y$.

    (1)　46.5°
    (2)　56.5°
    (3) 136.5°
    (4) 146.5°
    (5) 156.5°

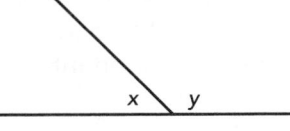

11. In the diagram below, which angles have the same measure as $\angle b$?

    (1) $\angle a$, $\angle d$, $\angle e$, and $\angle h$
    (2) $\angle c$, $\angle f$, and $\angle g$
    (3) $\angle c$, $\angle e$, and $\angle h$
    (4) only $\angle c$
    (5) only $\angle f$

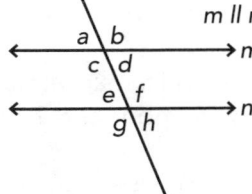

12. In isosceles triangle ABC, vertex angle $B = 94°$. What is the measure of each base angle of the triangle?

    (1)　43°
    (2)　86°
    (3)　94°
    (4)　96°
    (5) 137°

13. In the diagram below, $BC = 3$, $AC = 7$, and $DE = 5$. Find AE.

    (1)　8
    (2)　$9\frac{1}{3}$
    (3)　10
    (4)　$11\frac{2}{3}$
    (5)　13

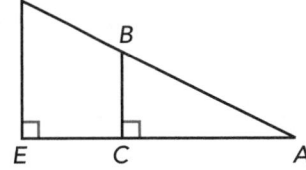

14. In the triangle below, $XZ = 16$ and $YZ = 12$. Find XY.

    (1)　14
    (2)　18
    (3)　20
    (4)　22
    (5)　24

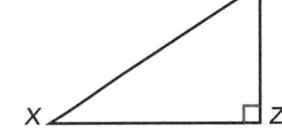

15. What is the slope of the line that passes through points A and B?

    (1)　$\frac{4}{5}$

    (2)　$\frac{5}{4}$

    (3)　$-\frac{5}{4}$

    (4)　$\frac{2}{3}$

    (5)　$-\frac{2}{3}$

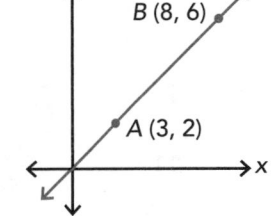

16. What is the measure of $\angle ABC$ in the diagram below?

    (1) 42°
    (2) 48°
    (3) 52°
    (4) 58°
    (5) 62°

PRETEST

Pretest Answer Grid, Part 3

1 _____

2 _____

3 _____

4 _____

5 _____

6	① ② ③ ④ ⑤	12	① ② ③ ④ ⑤
7	① ② ③ ④ ⑤	13	① ② ③ ④ ⑤
8	① ② ③ ④ ⑤	14	① ② ③ ④ ⑤
9	① ② ③ ④ ⑤	15	① ② ③ ④ ⑤
10	① ② ③ ④ ⑤	16	① ② ③ ④ ⑤
11	① ② ③ ④ ⑤		

PART 3

Algebra

Directions: Solve each problem.

1. Simplify $-9 - 3$.

2. Simplify $-8(+20)$.

3. Simplify $\frac{-6}{-8}$.

4. Solve for c in $4c - 7 = 13$.

5. Solve for m in $\frac{m}{2} - 11 = 3$.

Choose the correct answer to each problem.

6. The letter y represents Abdul's age now. Which expression represents Abdul's age in ten years?

    (1) $y - 10$
    (2) $y + 10$
    (3) $10y$
    (4) $10 - y$
    (5) $\frac{y}{10}$

7. Which expression represents the perimeter of triangle ABC?

    (1) $3x - 2$
    (2) $3x + 2$
    (3) $2x + 2$
    (4) $3x - 6$
    (5) $2x - 3$

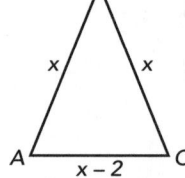

8. Shirley makes x dollars per hour for the first 40 hours of her workweek. She makes \$5 more for each hour beyond 40 hours. If Shirley works 47 hours, which expression represents the amount she makes in a week?

    (1) $47x$
    (2) $45x + 5$
    (3) $45x + 10$
    (4) $47x + 10$
    (5) $47x + 35$

9. Which expression represents the sum of a number and 7 divided by 3?

    (1) $\frac{x + 7}{3}$
    (2) $3(x + 7)$
    (3) $7(x + 3)$
    (4) $\frac{x + 3}{7}$
    (5) $3x + 7$

PRETEST

10. In a recent poll, registered voters were asked whether they would approve of a tax increase to build a new firehouse. The ratio of people who said yes to people who said no was 5:3. Altogether, 240 people were polled. How many people said yes?

(1) 180
(2) 150
(3) 120
(4) 90
(5) 60

11. A rectangle has a perimeter of 56 inches. The length is 4 inches greater than the width. Find the width of the rectangle in inches.

(1) 8
(2) 12
(3) 14
(4) 16
(5) 20

12. Which of the following is equal to $\sqrt{200}$?

(1) 50
(2) 100
(3) $10\sqrt{2}$
(4) $2\sqrt{10}$
(5) $20\sqrt{5}$

13. Which of the following is *not* a solution to $7a - 2 < 4a + 13$?

(1) $a = -4$
(2) $a = -3$
(3) $a = -2$
(4) $a = 4$
(5) $a = 6$

14. Which of the following is equal to the expression $4cd - 6c$?

(1) $4c(d - 6c)$
(2) $2c(d - 3)$
(3) $2c(2d - 6)$
(4) $2c(2d - 3)$
(5) $4c(d - 3c)$

15. What are the coordinates of the *y*-intercept if $y = 8x + 9$?

(1) $(9, 0)$
(2) $(0, 9)$
(3) $(-9, 0)$
(4) $(0, -9)$
(5) $(9, 9)$

16. For the equation $y = x^2 - 5x + 6$, what is the value of y when $x = 4$?

(1) 20
(2) 16
(3) 8
(4) 6
(5) 2

Answers are on page 11.

Answer Key

Part 1

Number Operations, Data Analysis, Statistics, and Probability, page 2

1. 1,610,000
$683 \rightarrow 700$
$2329 \rightarrow 2300$
$700 \times 2300 = 1,610,000$

2. 46.38
$46.3795 \rightarrow 46.38$

3. $2\frac{4}{9}$
$10\frac{1}{3} = 10\frac{3}{9} = 9\frac{3}{9} + \frac{9}{9} = 9\frac{12}{9}$
$-7\frac{8}{9} = \qquad\qquad 7\frac{8}{9}$
$\rule{3cm}{0.4pt}$
$\qquad\qquad\qquad\qquad 2\frac{4}{9}$

4. 26
$40\% = 0.4$
$0.4 \times 65 = 26$

5. 75%
$\frac{21}{28} = \frac{3}{4} = 75\%$

6. $210
$3.5\% = 0.035$
$1 \text{ yr } 6 \text{ mo} = 1\frac{6}{12} = 1.5 \text{ yr}$
$i = prt$
$i = \$4000 \times 0.035 \times 1.5 = \$210$

7. $10.15
$\$100 - 2(\$24.95) - \$39.95 = \$10.15$

8. 105 mi
$d = rt$
$d = 62 \times 1.5 + 24 \times 0.5$
$d = 93 + 12$
$d = 105$

9. 14,400
$120^2 = 120 \times 120 = 14,400$

10. $1.15 million $\$5.3 - \$4.15 = \$1.15$ million

11. 2:3
$56:84 = 8:12 = 2:3$

12. 9:10
$\$2 + \$18 = \$20$ total
spends:makes $= 18:20 = 9:10$

13. (4) 400,000 4 is in the hundred thousands place.

14. (2) 70
$82 \rightarrow 80$
$$80\overline{)5658} \quad \rightarrow \quad 70 + \text{remainder}$$

15. (3) $8 \times 9 + 8 \times 2$ This is the distributive property.

16. (2) 12($2467) 12 months $\times$ her monthly salary

17. (3) $\frac{12}{100}$ The other answers each equal $\frac{3}{4}$.

18. (5) $\frac{364}{7.5}$ $\text{mph} = \frac{\text{miles}}{\text{hours}} = \frac{364}{7.5}$

19. (4) 70 and 80 $70 \times 70 = 4900$ and
$80 \times 80 = 6400$

20. (2) 12(235 + 260) Add the number of people attending. Multiply by $12 per ticket.

21. (4) $2.13 $\$212.95 \div 100 = \$2.1295 \rightarrow \$2.13$

22. (3) $\frac{1}{3} \times \frac{9}{4}$ $\frac{1}{3} \times 2\frac{1}{4} = \frac{1}{3} \times \frac{9}{4}$

23. (4) 2.7×10^7
$27,000,000 = 2.7 \times 10^7$
The decimal point moves 7 places to the left.

24. (1) $2 - 0.25$ $\frac{1}{4} = 0.25$

25. (3) 1:5 staff salaries $= \$1.00 - \$0.80 = \$0.20$
$\$0.20:\$1.00 = 1:5$

26. (4) $4,000 $\frac{1}{5} \times \$20,000 = \$4,000$

27. (4) $106,000
$\$93,000 + \$98,000 + \$105,000 + \$128,000 = \$424,000$
$\$424,000 \div 4 = \$106,000$

28. (5) $\frac{1}{16}$ $\frac{\text{favorable}}{\text{possible}} = \frac{125}{2000} = \frac{5}{80} = \frac{1}{16}$

29. (4) $\frac{3}{5}$ $33\% + 27\% = 60\% = \frac{3}{5}$

30. (5) 3.0 $\frac{27\%}{9\%} = 3$

Part 2

Measurement and Geometry, page 6

1. $16\frac{2}{3}$ yd   1 yd = 3 ft

$$\frac{50}{3} = 16\frac{2}{3}$$

2. 8000 g   1 kg = 1000 g

$8 \times 1000 = 8000$ g

3. $1\frac{3}{8}$ in. $2\frac{1}{4} = 2\frac{2}{8} = 1\frac{2}{8} + \frac{8}{8} = 1\frac{10}{8}$

$$-\frac{7}{8} = \qquad \qquad \frac{7}{8}$$
$$1\frac{3}{8}$$

4. 135 mi $d = rt$

$d = 60 \times 2.25$

$d = 135$

5. (2) $\frac{6 \times 9}{12}$ 1 ft = 12 in.

$$\frac{6 \times 9}{12}$$

6. (4) 11 $P = 2l + 2w$

$P = 2(3.5) + 2(2.1)$

$P = 7 + 4.2$

$P = 11.2 \rightarrow 11$

7. (5) 480 $V = lwh$

$V = 12 \times 8 \times 5$

$V = 480$

8. (1) $\frac{23 \times 15}{2}$ $A = \frac{1}{2} \times 23 \times 15$

$A = \frac{23 \times 15}{2}$

9. (4) 310 $A = \pi r^2$

$A = 3.14 \times 10^2$

$A = 3.14 \times 100$

$A = 314 \rightarrow 310$

10. (3) 136.5° $\angle x + \angle y = 180°$

$180° - 43.5° = 136.5°$

11. (2) $\angle c$, $\angle f$, and $\angle g$ These three obtuse angles each have the same measure as $\angle b$. The other angles are acute.

12. (1) 43° x = one base angle

$x + x + 94° = 180°$

$2x = 86°$

$x = 43°$

13. (4) $11\frac{2}{3}$ $\frac{\text{height}}{\text{base}} = \frac{3}{7} = \frac{5}{x}$

$3x = 35$

$x = 11\frac{2}{3}$

14. (3) 20 $XY = \sqrt{12^2 + 16^2}$

$XY = \sqrt{144 + 256}$

$XY = \sqrt{400}$

$XY = 20$

15. (1) $\frac{4}{5}$ $\text{slope} = \frac{y_2 - y_1}{x_2 - x_1} = \frac{6 - 2}{8 - 3} = \frac{4}{5}$

16. (2) 48° $\angle ACB = 180° - 138° = 42°$

$\angle ABC = 180° - 90° - 42° = 48°$

Part 3

Algebra, page 8

1. -12 $-9 - 3 = -12$

2. -160 $-8(+20) = -160$

3. $+\frac{3}{4}$ $\frac{-6}{-8} = \frac{3}{4}$

4. $c = 5$ $4c - 7 = 13$

$4c = 20$

$c = 5$

5. $m = 28$ $\frac{m}{2} - 11 = 3$

$\frac{m}{2} = 14$

$m = 28$

6. (2) $y + 10$ "in 10 years" implies addition

7. (1) $3x - 2$ $P = x + x + x - 2 = 3x - 2$

8. (5) $47x + 35$ first 40 hours = $40x$
next 7 hours = $7(x + 5)$
total = $40x + 7(x + 5)$
$40x + 7x + 35$
$47x + 35$

9. (1) $\frac{x + 7}{3}$

10. (2) 150   yes = $5x$ and no = $3x$
$5x + 3x = 240$
$8x = 240$
$x = 30$
$5x = 5(30) = 150$

11. (2) 12   width = x
length = $x + 4$
$P = 2l + 2w$
$56 = 2(x + 4) + 2x$
$56 = 2x + 8 + 2x$
$56 = 4x + 8$
$48 = 4x$
$12 = x$

12. (3) $10\sqrt{2}$ $\sqrt{200} = \sqrt{100 \cdot 2} = 10\sqrt{2}$

13. (5) $a = 6$ $7a - 2 < 4a + 13$
$3a < 15$
$a < 5$
The other answers are less than 5.

14. (4) $2c(2d - 3)$ $4cd - 6c = 2c(2d - 3)$

15. (2) (0, 9)   When $x = 0$, $y = 8x + 9 = 8(0) + 9 = 9$

16. (5) 2   When $x = 4$, $y = x^2 - 5x + 6$
$y = 4^2 - 5(4) + 6$
$y = 16 - 20 + 6$
$y = 2$

PRETEST
Evaluation Chart

On the chart below, circle the number of the problems you got wrong. To the right of the problem numbers, you will find the sections and starting pages that cover the skills you need to solve the problems.

Pretest 1 Number Operations, Data Analysis, Statistics, and Probability

Problem	Section	Exercise Book Starting Page	GED Math Starting Page	Complete GED Starting Page
1, 9, 13, 14, 15, 19, 20	Whole Numbers	22	17	697
7, 8, 16, 17, 18	Word Problems	27	51	702
2, 10, 21, 23	Decimals	36	75	725
3, 17, 22, 24	Fractions	42	103	747
11, 12, 25, 26	Ratio and Proportion	48	137	785
4, 5, 6	Percent	55	149	793
27, 28, 29, 30	Data Analysis, Statistics, and Probability	70	197	809, 815

Pretest 2 Measurement and Geometry

Problem	Section	Exercise Book Starting Page	GED Math Starting Page	Complete GED Starting Page
1, 4, 5	Customary Measures	62	183	873
2	Metric Measures	62	186	879
3	Scales	62	190	889
6, 7, 8, 9	Perimeter, Circumference, Area, and Volume	82	234	897
10, 11	Angles	82	223	904
12, 13, 16	Triangles	82	259	907
15	Slope	82	331	860
14	Pythagorean Relationship	82	371	908

Pretest 3 Algebra

Problem	Section	Exercise Book Starting Page	GED Math Starting Page	Complete GED Starting Page
1, 2, 3	Signed Numbers	94	281	775
6, 7, 8, 9	Expressions	94	292	836
4, 5	Equations	94	294	838
10, 11	Word Problems	94	315	841
13	Inequalities	94	304	852
12, 14	Factoring	103	339	864
15	Coordinate Plane	103	323	854
16	Quadratic Equations	103	346	863

Using a Calculator

GED Mathematics pp. 28–29 and throughout
Complete GED throughout

The GED Mathematics Test permits the use of a scientific calculator on half of the test. The Casio *fx*-260 SOLAR is the only calculator permitted with the test.

To turn on the calculator, press the **ON** key at the upper right or the red **AC** key. A small "DEG" will appear at the top center of the display and "0." will appear at the right of the display.

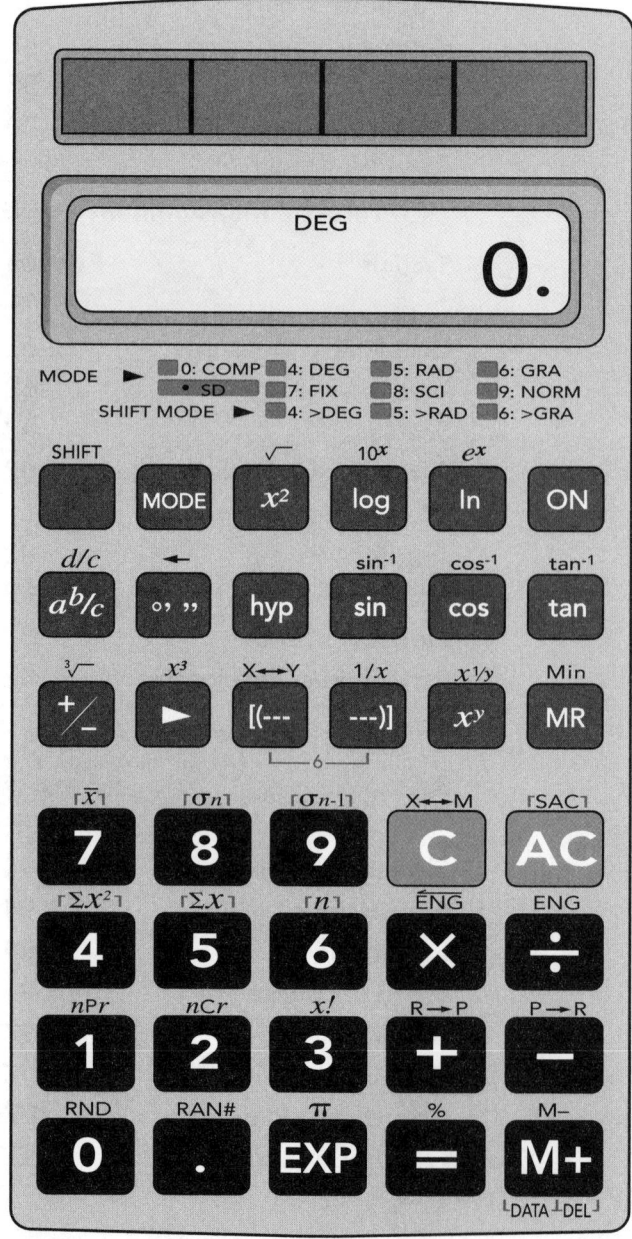

Basic Whole-Number Operations

To perform addition, subtraction, multiplication, and division operations, enter the numbers and operation signs. Then press ⬛**=** when you finish.

Example 1   Solve 17 + 26 on a calculator.

Press **1** **7** **+** **2** **6** **=** .
The answer is ⎿____43.____⏌ .

Example 2   Find 76 − 29 on a calculator.

Press **7** **6** **−** **2** **9** **=** .
The answer is ⎿____47.____⏌ .

Example 3   Solve 35 × 9 on a calculator.

Press **3** **5** **×** **9** **=** .
The answer is ⎿____315.____⏌ .

Example 4   Divide 68$\overline{)2312}$ with a calculator.

Press **2** **3** **1** **2** **÷** **6** **8** **=** .
The answer is ⎿____34.____⏌ .

Powers and Roots

To find the second power of a number, enter the number. Then press the **x²** key.

Example 1   Solve 18^2 on a calculator.

Press **1** **8** **x²** .
The answer is ⎿____324.____⏌ .

To find the square root of a number, enter the number. Then press the **SHIFT** key followed by the **x²** key. The **SHIFT** key changes the next key that you press to a second function. For the **x²** key, the second function is the square root.

Example 2   Find $\sqrt{6724}$ on a calculator.

Press **6** **7** **2** **4** **SHIFT** **x²** .

The answer is ⎿____82.____⏌ .

Decimals

To enter a decimal point, press the ⬤•⬤ key.

Example 1   Solve 3.2 − 1.56 on a calculator.

Press ⬤3⬤ ⬤•⬤ ⬤2⬤ ⬤−⬤ ⬤1⬤ ⬤•⬤ ⬤5⬤ ⬤6⬤ ⬤=⬤.

The answer is ⎡ 1.64 ⎤.

Example 2   Find 4.8 × 0.75 on a calculator.

Press ⬤4⬤ ⬤•⬤ ⬤8⬤ ⬤×⬤ ⬤•⬤ ⬤7⬤ ⬤5⬤ ⬤=⬤.

The answer is ⎡ 3.6 ⎤.

You may have to round calculator answers to decimal problems.

Example 3   Solve 4.6 ÷ 3.5 = on a calculator. Show the answer to the nearest tenth.

Press ⬤4⬤ ⬤•⬤ ⬤6⬤ ⬤÷⬤ ⬤3⬤ ⬤•⬤ ⬤5⬤ ⬤=⬤.

The answer on the display is ⎡ 1.314285714 ⎤.

To the nearest tenth, the answer is 1.3.

Fractions

The key for entering a fraction or a mixed number is ⬤a b/c⬤.

Example 1   Reduce $\frac{84}{96}$ on a calculator.

Press ⬤8⬤ ⬤4⬤ ⬤a b/c⬤ ⬤9⬤ ⬤6⬤ ⬤=⬤.

The answer on the display is ⎡ 7⌐8. ⎤, which means $\frac{7}{8}$.

Example 2   Find $1\frac{1}{2} + 2\frac{3}{4}$ on a calculator.

Press ⬤1⬤ ⬤a b/c⬤ ⬤1⬤ ⬤a b/c⬤ ⬤2⬤ ⬤+⬤ ⬤2⬤ ⬤a b/c⬤ ⬤3⬤ ⬤a b/c⬤ ⬤4⬤ ⬤=⬤.

The answer on the display is ⎡ 4⌐1⌐4. ⎤, which means $4\frac{1}{4}$.

(*Note:* The calculator is an awkward tool for solving most fraction problems. However, the calculator is a convenient tool for reducing fractions.)

Grouping Symbols

The keys for grouping calculations are 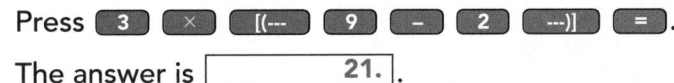. In the first example, when the expression in parentheses is to be multiplied by a number, the ✕ key (multiplication sign) is pressed between the number and the parenthesis [(--- key.

Example 1 Solve 3(9 − 2) on a calculator.

Press 3 ✕ [(--- 9 − 2 ---)] = .
The answer is ⎣   21. ⎦.

The Casio *fx*-260 calculator has no symbol for the extended division bar. You will need to use the open parenthesis [(--- and the close parenthesis ---)] keys to indicate an operation that is to be calculated first. In the next example, notice how the numbers that are grouped above the fraction bar, 14 − 8, are grouped with the [(--- and ---)] keys on the calculator.

Example 2 Use a calculator to find the value of $\frac{14-8}{3}$.

Press 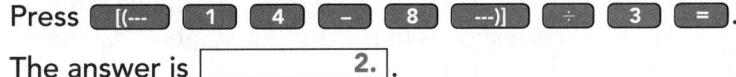.
The answer is ⎣   2. ⎦.

Negative Numbers

The numbers entered on a calculator are assumed to be positive. To change a number to a negative, press the +/− key. Notice that the +/− key is pressed *after* the number although a minus sign is written to the left of a negative number in algebra.

Example 1 Solve 3(−12) on a calculator.

Press 3 ✕ 1 2 +/− = .
The answer is ⎣   −36. ⎦.

Example 2 Solve $\frac{-54}{-9}$ on a calculator.

Press 5 4 +/− ÷ 9 +/− = .
The answer is ⎣   6. ⎦, which is assumed to be positive.

Example 3 Solve $\frac{-32}{8}$ on a calculator.

Press 3 2 +/− ÷ 8 = .
The answer is ⎣   −4. ⎦.

Using the Number Grid and the Coordinate Plane Grid

GED Mathematics pages 45–46, 95–97, 129–132
Complete GED throughout

The answer sheets for the GED Mathematics Test include several number grids on which you will be asked to mark whole number, decimal, or fraction answers. Each grid contains five blank boxes above five columns of numbers and symbols.

To mark an answer on a number grid, first write the correct answer in the blank boxes. Use a separate column for each digit or symbol. Then, below each column, fill in one circle that corresponds to the digit or symbol that you wrote on top.

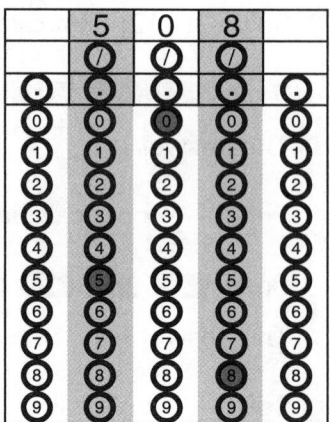

Whole Number Answers

Example   Mark the number 508 on an answer grid.

Below are three correctly filled in grids for the number 508. On the first grid, the digits start at the left. On the second grid, the digits are centered. On the third grid, the digits occupy the right-most columns.

Correct Answer   Correct Answer   Correct Answer

Below are two *incorrectly* filled in grids for the number 508. On the first grid, the circles are not filled in. On the second grid, all of the circles in the first column were filled in.

Incorrect Answer   Incorrect Answer

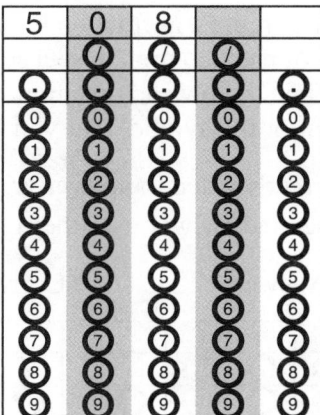 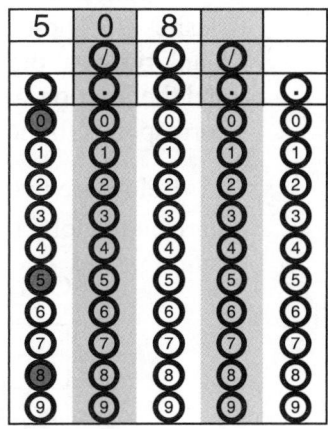

Decimal Answers

Example   Mark the number 12.7 on an answer grid.

Notice that the third row of boxes in an answer grid contains circled decimal points. Write the answer 12.7 in the blank boxes at the top of each column. Use a separate column for each digit and the decimal point. Then, below each column, fill in one circle that corresponds to the digit or the symbol that you wrote at the top.

Below are two correctly filled in answer grids for 12.7. The first answer starts at the left. The second answer uses the right side of the grid.

Correct Answer   Correct Answer

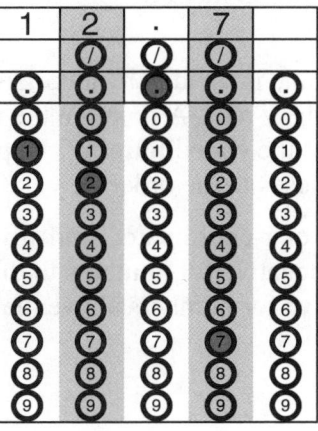

Fraction Answers

Example   Mark the fraction $\frac{5}{16}$ on an answer grid.

Notice that the second row of boxes in an answer grid contains three slashes (/). These slashes represent fraction bars. Write the answer 5/16 in the blank boxes at the top of each column. Use a separate column for each digit and the fraction bar. Then, below each column, fill in one circle that corresponds to the digit or the symbol that you wrote at the top.

Below are two correctly filled in answer grids for $\frac{5}{16}$. The first answer starts at the left. The second answer uses the right side of the grid.

Correct Answer   Correct Answer

The Coordinate Plane Grid

On the GED Mathematics Test you will see coordinate plane grids with small circles where you can mark the position of a point on the coordinate plane.

The coordinate plane is divided by a horizontal line called the **x-axis** and a vertical line called the **y-axis.** A point on the plane can be identified by a pair of numbers called the **coordinates** of the point. The coordinates are written inside parentheses in the order (x, y).

The first number, or x-coordinate, is positive for numbers to the right of the vertical axis and negative for numbers to the left. The second number, or y-coordinate, is positive for numbers above the horizontal axis and negative for numbers below.

Example 1   Mark the point $(-3, 4)$ on a coordinate plane grid.

The point $(-3, 4)$ is 3 units *left* of the vertical axis and 4 units *above* the horizontal axis.

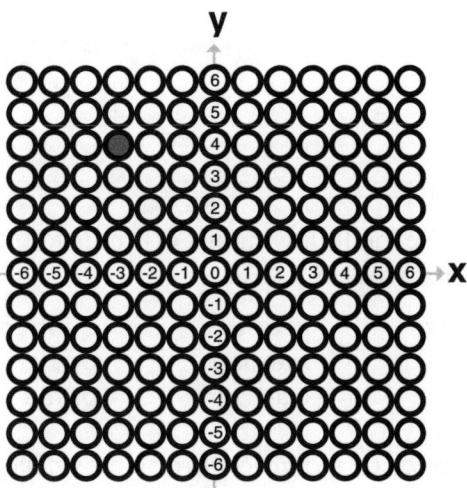

Example 2   Mark the point $(5, -2)$ on a coordinate plane grid.

The point $(5, -2)$ is 5 units *right* of the vertical axis and 2 units *below* the horizontal axis.

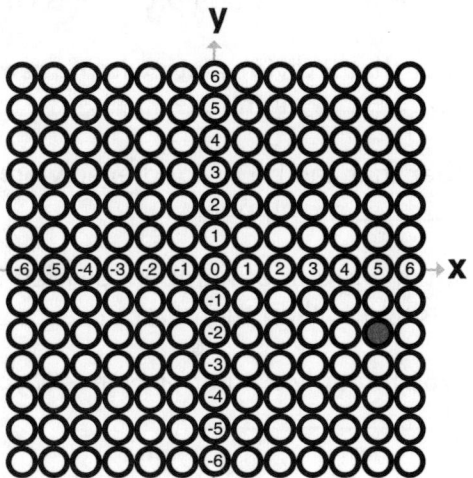

 Go to **www.GEDMath.com** for additional practice and instruction!

Chapter 1

Whole Numbers

GED Mathematics pp. 17–50
Complete GED pp. 697–701, 711–713

Basic Skills

Directions: Use the following list of words to fill in the blanks for problems 1–10.

difference	product	quotient	sum
mean	median	power	square root
even	odd	prime	consecutive

1. The answer to a division problem is called the _____.

2. The answer to a subtraction problem is called the _____.

3. The answer to a multiplication problem is called the _____.

4. The answer to an addition problem is called the _____.

5. A number that 2 divides into with no remainder is called an _____ number.

6. A number that can be divided evenly only by 1 and itself is called a _____ number.

7. The sum of a group of numbers divided by the number of numbers in the group is called the _____.

8. When you multiply a number by itself, you raise the number to the second _____.

9. When you add 1 to a number, you find the next _____ number.

10. The middle value for a group of numbers is called the _____.

Solve each problem.

11. Circle the even numbers in this list. 8 13 20 27 35

12. Circle the odd numbers in this list. 9 14 23 31 42

13. List the prime numbers between 15 and 30.

14. In the number 25,308, which digit is in the ten thousands place?

15. In the number 846,571, which digit is in the thousands place?

16. Round each number in this list to the nearest ten.
    83   129   3472   5019

17. Round each number in this list to the nearest hundred.
    274   6386   10,987   4926

18. Find the difference between 9078 and 8949.

19. What is the product of 8300 and 46?

20. Find the quotient of 7291 ÷ 23.

21. For the problem 88 + 721 + 4068, round each number to the nearest ten. Then add the rounded numbers.

22. For the problem 168,274 − 43,916, round each number to the nearest thousand. Then subtract the rounded numbers.

23. For the problem 748 × 59, round each number to the left-most digit. Then multiply the rounded numbers.

24. Find the quotient, to the nearest hundred, of 33,540 divided by 48.

25. Evaluate 17^2.

26. What is $\sqrt{400}$?

27. Evaluate the expression 3 × 17 − 9 × 2.

28. Find the next term in the sequence 1, 6, 4, 9, 7. . .

29. Find the mean for the numbers 71, 46, 98, and 53.

30. What is the median for the numbers in the last problem?

Answers are on page 131.

GED PRACTICE

PART I

Directions: You may use a calculator to solve the following problems. For problems 1–3, mark each answer on the corresponding number grid.

1. What is the quotient of 220,320 divided by 720?

2. Round each number below to the nearest hundred. Then find the sum of the rounded numbers. 1285, 817, and 2073

3. Round 92 and 79 to the nearest ten. Then find the product of the rounded numbers.

Choose the correct answer to each problem.

4. Which of the following is equivalent to 18^3?

   (1) $18 + 18 + 18$
   (2) 3×18
   (3) $18 - 18 - 18$
   (4) $18 \times 18 \times 18$
   (5) $18 \div 3$

5. What is 48^2?

   (1)   96
   (2)   960
   (3)   2304
   (4)   3024
   (5)   9600

6. What is the next term in the sequence 5, 15, 10, 30, 25 . . .

   (1) 30
   (2) 40
   (3) 50
   (4) 75
   (5) 90

GED PRACTICE

7. Simplify the expression $\frac{4 \times 30}{26 - 16}$.

(1) 10
(2) 12
(3) 20
(4) 24
(5) 30

8. Lou took five math tests. His scores were 81, 78, 93, 86, and 72. What was his median score?

(1) 78
(2) 80
(3) 81
(4) 82
(5) 86

9. Maria's office bought new equipment in 1998. The table below shows the estimated value of the equipment each year since it was purchased. If the pattern continued, what was the value of the equipment in 2002?

Year	1998	1999	2000	2001	2002
Value in $	3000	2600	2200	1800	?

(1) $1400
(2) $1380
(3) $1200
(4) $1140
(5) $1000

10. Bettina works weekends as a waitress. On Friday she made $219 in tips. On Saturday she made $217, and on Sunday she made $185. Find her average daily tips for the weekend.

(1) $201
(2) $207
(3) $210
(4) $217
(5) $219

PART II

Directions: Solve the following problems without a calculator.

11. The answer to 2,764 + 1,814 + 16,285 is between which of the following pairs of numbers?

(1) 5,000 and 10,000
(2) 10,000 and 15,000
(3) 15,000 and 20,000
(4) 20,000 and 25,000
(5) 25,000 and 30,000

12. The answer to 83^2 is between which of the following pairs of numbers?

(1) 1600 and 2500
(2) 2500 and 3600
(3) 3600 and 4900
(4) 4900 and 6400
(5) 6400 and 8100

13. Which of the following is the same as 6(5 + 7)?

(1) $6 \times 5 \times 7$
(2) 5(6 + 7)
(3) 7(6 + 5)
(4) $6 \times 5 + 6 \times 7$
(5) 6 + 5 + 7

14. The square root of 5476 is between which of the following pairs of numbers?

(1) 50 and 60
(2) 60 and 70
(3) 70 and 80
(4) 80 and 90
(5) 90 and 100

15. Which of the following is *not* a factor of 40?

(1) 5
(2) 8
(3) 10
(4) 20
(5) 25

For problems 16 and 17, mark each answer on the corresponding number grid.

16. Evaluate the expression $\frac{10^3 - 10^2}{8 - 3}$.

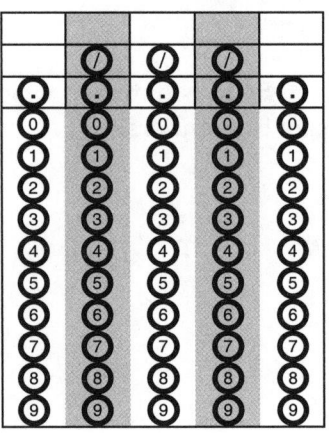

17. Evaluate the expression $9(27 + 14)$.

18. If *r* represents the square root of 5184, which of the following is true?

(1) $r \times r = 5184$
(2) $r + r = 5184$
(3) $r - r = 5184$
(4) $r \div r = 5184$
(5) $\frac{r}{2} = 5184$

19. In the last census, the population of New Mexico was 1,819,046. What was the population rounded to the nearest ten thousand?

(1) 2,000,000
(2) 1,820,000
(3) 1,819,000
(4) 1,810,000
(5) 1,800,000

20. You know Yolanda's scores on four Spanish quizzes. Which of the following best describes the way to find her mean or average score?

(1) Add the scores.
(2) Subtract the lowest score from the highest score.
(3) Find half of each score and add the results.
(4) Add the scores and divide by four.
(5) Look for the score with the middle value.

Answers are on page 131.

Chapter 2

Word Problems

GED Mathematics pp. 51–74
Complete GED pp. 702–710

Basic Skills

Directions: For problems 1–10, first identify the operation or operations that you need to use to solve each problem. Write *add, subtract, multiply, divide,* or some combination of these operations. Then solve each problem.

1. In 1990 the population of Northport was 12,783. In 2000 the population of Northport was 14,296. How many more people lived in Northport in 2000 than in 1990?

   Operation:

   Solution:

2. The population of Middletown was 46,597 in 2000. By 2001 the population of Middletown had increased by 948 people. What was the population of Middletown in 2001?

   Operation:

   Solution:

3. A souvenir T-shirt sells for $7.99. Find the price of a dozen T-shirts.

   Operation:

   Solution:

4. Frances paid $5.37 for 3 pounds of pork. What was the price of 1 pound of pork?

   Operation:

   Solution:

5. Sam bought 8 gallons of gasoline that cost $1.85 a gallon. How much change did he get from $20?

   Operation:

   Solution:

6. To get to his daughter's house, Rex drove 265 miles on Friday, 418 miles on Saturday, and 170 miles on Sunday. How far did Rex drive to get to his daughter's house?

   Operation:

   Solution:

7. Mel and Pam need $17,500 as a down payment for a house. So far they have saved $14,300. How much more do they need for the down payment?

   Operation:

   Solution:

8. Shirley drove 221 miles on 13 gallons of gasoline. Find her average gas mileage in miles per gallon.

   Operation:

   Solution:

9. Phil had scores of 65, 88, 79, and 92 on math quizzes last semester. Find his average score on the quizzes.

   Operation:

   Solution:

10. Lorraine's gross weekly salary is $682.40. Her employer deducts $102.36 from her check each week. Find Lorraine's net weekly salary.

    Operation:

    Solution:

For problems 11–15, choose the correct method for solving each problem.

11. You know Mr. Chan's monthly income, and you know Mrs. Chan's monthly income. How do you find their combined income?

    (1) Divide the larger income by the smaller income.
    (2) Subtract their incomes.
    (3) Add their incomes.

12. You know how many yards of cloth a tailor needs to make a jacket, and you know how many yards of material he has. How do you find the number of jackets he can make from the amount of cloth that he has?

    (1) Divide the amount of cloth the tailor has by the amount he needs for one jacket.
    (2) Multiply the amount of cloth the tailor needs for one jacket by the total amount of cloth the tailor has.
    (3) Subtract the amount of cloth the tailor needs for one jacket from the total amount of cloth the tailor has.

13. You know the average speed that Marcia walks, and you know the length of time it takes her to walk to work. How do you find the total distance that Marcia walks to work?

    (1) Add her average speed to the time she walks.
    (2) Multiply her average speed by the time she walks.
    (3) Divide her average speed by the time she walks.

14. You know the price of a movie ticket, and you know the number of seats in a movie theater. How do you find the total amount paid for movie tickets when the theater is full?

    (1) Multiply the price of a ticket by the number of seats.
    (2) Divide the number of seats by the price of a ticket.
    (3) Subtract the price of a ticket from the number of seats.

15. You know Max's weight last year, and you know the amount of weight he has lost since then. How do you find Max's current weight?

    (1) Add the weight he lost to his weight last year.
    (2) Divide his weight last year by the weight he lost.
    (3) Subtract the weight he lost from his weight last year.

For problems 16–20, each problem has more numerical information than is necessary to solve the problem. First identify the unnecessary information. Then solve each problem.

16. Eight co-workers each paid $20 to buy lottery tickets. They agreed to share any winnings equally. The co-workers won a prize of $10,000. How much did each worker get?

    Unnecessary information:

    Solution:

17. The Andersons pay $814 a month for their mortgage and $117 a month for their car. How much do they pay in a year for their mortgage?

    Unnecessary information:

    Solution:

18. A volunteer fire department mailed 1000 requests for donations to renovate their firehouse. The firemen received $14,720 from 640 donors. What was the average donation?

    Unnecessary information:

    Solution:

19. José loaded 3 crates weighing a total of 2750 pounds onto an elevator that can safely carry 3000 pounds. How much more weight can the elevator carry?

    Unnecessary information:

    Solution:

20. In 1997 the Roberts family spent $790 to heat their house. In 1999 they spent $1265, and in 2001 they spent $1410. By how much did the cost of heating their house rise from 1997 to 2001?

    Unnecessary information:

    Solution:

For problems 21–25, choose the expression for calculating the best estimate to each problem. Then find the exact answer.

21. A train traveled for 18 hours at an average speed of 72 mph. How far did the train travel?

    (1) 100 × 12
    (2) 70 × 20
    (3) 80 × 10

    Solution:

22. Find the cost of four pairs of children's jeans that cost $14.79 each.

    (1) 4 × $10
    (2) 4 × $12
    (3) 4 × $15

    Solution:

23. The total distance from Mary's house to her summer cabin is 719 miles. On her way to the cabin, Mary stopped for lunch after driving 189 miles. How many more miles did she need to drive to reach the cabin?

    (1) 700 − 200
    (2) 800 − 200
    (3) 1000 − 100

    Solution:

24. On Friday 2683 people attended a basketball tournament, and on Saturday 3127 people attended the tournament. What was the average attendance for those days?

    (1) $\dfrac{2000 + 3000}{2}$

    (2) $\dfrac{3000 + 3000}{2}$

    (3) $\dfrac{4000 + 3000}{2}$

    Solution:

25. When Jack started as a part-time worker at Apex, he made $6,945 a year. Now, as a manager, he makes $41,670 a year. His salary now is how many times his starting salary?

    (1) $\dfrac{\$42,000}{\$7,000}$

    (2) $\dfrac{\$40,000}{\$5,000}$

    (3) $\dfrac{\$40,000}{\$8,000}$

    Solution:

Answers are on page 132.

GED PRACTICE

PART I

Directions: Use a calculator to solve the following problems. For problems 1–3, mark each answer on the corresponding number grid.

1. Driving on highways, Victoria gets an average of 28 miles on 1 gallon of gasoline. How far can she drive on the highway with a full tank that holds 14 gallons of gasoline?

2. At the Elton Machine Corporation there are 228 employees in the 8:00 A.M. to 4:00 P.M. shift, 197 employees on the 4:00 P.M. to midnight shift, and 146 employees on the midnight to 8:00 A.M. shift. Altogether, how many people work at Elton Machine?

3. A printer has to ship new telephone books to 14,112 residential customers. The books are packed in bundles of 12. How many bundles are required to ship the entire order?

Choose the correct answer to each problem.

4. In a recent year the most popular Internet guide to Philadelphia had 181,000 visitors. The second-most popular guide had 79,000 visitors. How many more people visited the most popular site than visited the second-most popular site?

   (1)   92,000
   (2)   98,000
   (3) 102,000
   (4) 108,000
   (5) 112,000

5. A cartridge for a laser printer costs $73.99 for one or $71.79 each if you buy three or more. Find the cost of six cartridges at the discounted price.

   (1) $430.74
   (2) $433.94
   (3) $437.85
   (4) $443.94
   (5) $440.74

6. According to the Census Bureau, the population of Seattle increased from 4,987,000 in 1990 to 5,894,000 in 2000. By how many people did the population increase from 1990 to 2000?

   (1) 197,000
   (2) 907,000
   (3) 917,000
   (4) 927,000
   (5) 987,000

7. Joan takes care of her father's bills. At the beginning of April, his checking account had a balance of $1084.27. Joan paid her father's rent of $475.00. Then she deposited his pension check for $396.40. Finally, she paid the telephone bill for $49.58. How much was left in the account after she paid the phone bill?

   (1) $ 956.09
   (2) $1005.67
   (3) $1056.09
   (4) $1105.67
   (5) $1136.09

8. To build an addition to a community athletic facility, a town needs to raise $1,500,000. So far the residents have raised $768,520 toward the new construction. How much more do they need?

   (1) $831,480
   (2) $768,520
   (3) $731,480
   (4) $668,520
   (5) $631,480

9. Maxine can type 65 words per minute. How many minutes will she need to type a document that contains 2600 words?

   (1) 25
   (2) 30
   (3) 35
   (4) 40
   (5) 45

10. Find the total cost of 3 pounds of beef at $3.90 a pound and 4 pounds of fish at $7.89 a pound.

    (1) $27.30
    (2) $29.43
    (3) $31.56
    (4) $43.26
    (5) $55.23

PART II

Directions: Solve the following problems without a calculator. For problems 11 and 12, mark each answer on the corresponding number grid.

11. From September through May, the publishers of the *Shoretown Daily News* print 2850 copies of their newspaper daily. During the summer months, they print 6000 copies daily. How many more copies are printed each day in the summer than are printed each day for the rest of the year?

12. Melanie bought a new dining table and a set of chairs. She purchased the furniture on an installment plan by paying $200 down and $36 a month for a full year. What total price, in dollars, did Melanie pay for the furniture?

Choose the correct answer to each problem.

13. The table shows the number of registrations in the Midvale night school classes for three different years. The number of registrations in 2001 was about how many times the number of registrations in 1991?

Year	1991	1996	2001
Registrations	203	420	615

(1) about the same
(2) about 2 times
(3) about 3 times
(4) about 4 times
(5) about 5 times

14. Selma drove for 4 hours on an interstate highway at an average speed of 68 mph and then for another hour in a city at an average speed of 17 mph. Which expression represents the total distance Selma drove in those 5 hours?

(1) $68 \times 4 - 17$
(2) $68 \times 4 + 17$
(3) 68×5
(4) $5(68 + 17)$
(5) $5(68 - 17)$

15. In a recent year the number of households in Baltimore was 255,772. To estimate the actual population, a local politician assumed that the average household was about three people. Assuming that the politician was correct, which of the following is the best guess of the population of Baltimore that year?

(1) about 2 million
(2) about 1 million
(3) about 750,000
(4) about 500,000
(5) about 250,000

16. According to a study, in 1992 the average resident of Atlanta lost 25 hours a year while waiting in traffic jams. In 1999 the average resident of Atlanta lost 53 hours while waiting in traffic jams. The average Atlanta resident lost how many more hours in traffic jams in 1999 than in 1992?

(1) 12
(2) 18
(3) 20
(4) 23
(5) 28

Problems 17–19 refer to the following information.

One-Way Fare from New York to	
Chicago	$152
Honolulu	$359
Los Angeles	$219
Paris	$304

17. According to the list, how much is round-trip airfare from New York to Honolulu?

(1) $304
(2) $359
(3) $438
(4) $608
(5) $718

18. Round-trip airfare from New York to Los Angeles is how much more than round-trip airfare from New York to Chicago?

(1) $ 67
(2) $134
(3) $140
(4) $167
(5) $304

19. One-way airfare from New York to Paris is how many times the cost of one-way airfare from New York to Chicago?

(1) the same
(2) 2 times
(3) 3 times
(4) 4 times
(5) 5 times

20. Rick drove 500 miles in 13 hours. To the nearest ten, what was his average driving speed in miles per hour?

(1) 20
(2) 30
(3) 40
(4) 50
(5) 60

Answers are on page 133.

 Go to **www.GEDMath.com** for additional practice and instruction!

Chapter 3

Decimals

Basic Skills

Directions: Solve each problem.

1. Circle the digit in the tenths place in each number.
   2.6   3.714   18.9

2. Circle the digit in the hundredths place in each number.
   0.45   2.986   12.065

3. Circle the digit in the thousandths place in each number.
   0.1265   0.0078   2.1294

For problems 4–6, fill in the blanks with the correct decimal name.

4. 0.16 = sixteen _____ .

5. 3.2 = three and two _____ .

6. 12.019 = twelve and nineteen _____ .

7. Rewrite the number 00902.7350 and omit unnecessary zeros.

8. Round each number to the nearest tenth.
   0.38   2.419   36.083

9. Round each number to the nearest hundredth.
   1.777   0.0284   0.199

10. Round each number to the nearest unit.
    13.099   5.702   128.66

11. Write eight hundredths as a decimal.

12. Write fourteen and seven thousandths as a decimal.

13. In $4.37 which digit is in the tenths place?

14. Find the sum of 2.15, 16.72, and 0.368.

15. For the last problem, round each number to the nearest tenth. Then find the sum of the rounded numbers.

16. Subtract 3.42 from 28.726.

17. For the last problem, round each number to the nearest unit. Then subtract the rounded numbers.

18. Find the product of 32.6 and 5.4.

19. For the last problem, round each number to the nearest unit. Then find the product of the rounded numbers.

20. What is $\frac{0.56}{7}$?

21. Divide 4.56 by 12.

22. Find the quotient of 2.844 divided by 0.36.

23. What is $15 \div 9$ to the nearest tenth?

24. What is $25 \div 30$ to the nearest hundredth?

25. What is $(1.4)^2$?

26. Evaluate $(0.25)^2$.

27. What is $\sqrt{0.0036}$?

28. Evaluate $\sqrt{0.49}$.

29. Write 5.9×10^6 as a whole number.

30. Write 480,000,000 in scientific notation.

Answers are on page 134.

PART I

Directions: You may use a calculator to solve the following problems. For problems 1–3, mark each answer on the corresponding number grid.

1. There are 7.11 million Internet users in New York City and 5.34 million Internet users in Los Angeles. How many more million Internet users are there in New York City than in Los Angeles?

2. A wooden crate weighs 19.2 pounds, and a generator that will be shipped in the crate weighs 73.9 pounds. What is the combined weight, in pounds, of the crate and the generator?

3. Sam drove 306 miles on 14 gallons of gasoline. To the nearest tenth, how many miles did he drive on one gallon of gasoline?

Choose the correct answer to each problem.

4. A can contains 0.538 kilogram of beans. If half of the beans go into a food processor, what is the weight, in kilograms, of beans in the food processor?

   (1) 0.038
   (2) 0.20
   (3) 0.269
   (4) 0.50
   (5) 0.538

5. What is the cost of 0.87 pound of cheese at $5.79 a pound?

   (1) $4.05
   (2) $4.34
   (3) $4.64
   (4) $5.04
   (5) $5.16

6. A batting average is the number of hits a baseball player gets divided by the number of times he is at bat. The quotient is rounded to the nearest thousandth. Jake was at bat 80 times and got 27 hits. What was his batting average?

   (1) .270
   (2) .338
   (3) .400
   (4) .500
   (5) .540

7. Paula drove at an average speed of 52 mph for 0.75 hour. How many miles did she drive?

   (1) 75
   (2) 52
   (3) 43
   (4) 39
   (5) 31

8. Joan makes $19.60 an hour for overtime work. One week her paycheck included $68.60 for overtime. How many hours did she work overtime that week?

   (1) 2.5
   (2) 3
   (3) 3.5
   (4) 4
   (5) 4.5

9. Find the mean weight, in kilograms, of three parcels that weigh 1.2 kg, 2.55 kg, and 2.7 kg.

   (1) 2.15
   (2) 2.35
   (3) 2.5
   (4) 2.65
   (5) 2.7

10. If a jar contains 0.65 kilogram of plums, how many jars can be filled if you have 20 kilograms of plums?

    (1) 30
    (2) 32
    (3) 34
    (4) 36
    (5) 38

For problems 11 and 12, refer to the following information.

Rates for Electricity	
Commercial	15.0883¢ per kilowatt hour (kWh)
Residential	13.0966¢ per kilowatt hour (kWh)

11. Jason has a cabinet-making shop next to his house. He pays the commercial rate for the electricity that he uses in his shop and the residential rate for the electricity that he uses in his house. One month he used 290 kilowatt hours of electricity in his shop. Find the cost of the electricity that he used in his shop that month.

    (1) $25.61
    (2) $28.01
    (3) $37.98
    (4) $43.76
    (5) $45.82

12. What is the difference between the cost of 100 kilowatt hours of electricity at the commercial rate and 100 kilowatt hours of electricity at the residential rate?

    (1) $0.99
    (2) $1.99
    (3) $2.99
    (4) $4.90
    (5) $9.90

PART II

Directions: Solve the following problems without a calculator. For problems 13 and 14, mark each answer on the corresponding number grid.

13. In 1987, 964.5 million acres of land were used for farming in the U.S. In 1997, the number of acres used for farming was 931.8 million. From 1987 to 1997, the total number of acres used for farming dropped by how many million?

14. What is the total weight, in pounds, of 100 cans of tomatoes if each can weighs 2.189 pounds?

Choose the correct answer to each problem.

15. From a 30-foot-long nylon rope, Tim cut two pieces, each 12.3 meters long. Which expression represents the length, in meters, of the remaining piece of rope?

(1) $30 - 2(12.3)$
(2) $2(30 - 12.3)$
(3) $2(30) - 12.3$
(4) $30 - 12.3$
(5) $30 + 2(12.3)$

16. The population of Central County rose from 1.05 million people in 1992 to 1.8 million people in 2002. How many more people lived in Central County in 2002 than in 1992?

(1) 7,500,000
(2) 6,500,000
(3)   750,000
(4)   650,000
(5)   250,000

17. The list below tells the lengths, in meters, of five plastic tubes. Arrange the tubes in order from shortest to longest.

A   0.4 m
B   0.54 m
C   0.45 m
D   0.05 m
E   0.054 m

(1) A, D, E, C, B
(2) D, E, A, C, B
(3) B, C, A, D, E
(4) D, E, C, B, A
(5) A, E, C, D, B

18. The illustration shows two boards labeled A and B that are connected by a screw that is 1.875 inches long. How many inches into board A is the screw?

(1) 0.875
(2) 1.0
(3) 1.125
(4) 1.25
(5) 1.5

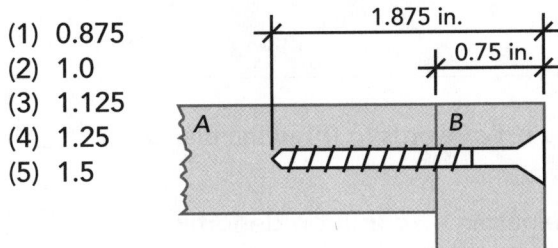

19. Hannah bought 2.5 pounds of cheese that cost $4.99 per pound. Which of the following represents the change in dollars and cents that Hannah should get from $20?

(1) $20(4.99 - 2.5)$
(2) $4.99 - 2.5(20)$
(3) $2.5 - 20(4.99)$
(4) $2.5(4.99) - 20$
(5) $20 - 2.5(4.99)$

For problems 20 and 21, refer to the information below.

Average Price of a Gallon of Gasoline (summer 2001)	
California	$2.02
Michigan	$1.90
Alabama	$1.56
Georgia	$1.49

20. The gasoline tank in Sandy's car holds 20 gallons. Using the rates listed above, how much would it cost Sandy to fill her tank at the average price of gasoline in Michigan?

(1) $29.80
(2) $31.20
(3) $38.00
(4) $40.40
(5) $48.00

21. According to the list, how much more do 10 gallons of gasoline cost at the average price in California than 10 gallons at the average price in Georgia?

(1) $1.20
(2) $3.40
(3) $4.10
(4) $4.60
(5) $5.30

22. In the orbit of the planet Neptune, its greatest distance from the sun is 2,822,000,000 miles. Represent this number of miles in scientific notation.

(1) 2.822×10^{10}
(2) 2.822×10^{9}
(3) 2.822×10^{8}
(4) 2.822×10^{7}
(5) 2.822×10^{6}

23. According to the 2000 census, the combined population of the 100 largest cities in the U.S. was 5.84×10^{7}. Which of the following equals the population of the 100 largest cities?

(1) 584,000,000
(2) 58,400,000
(3) 5,840,000
(4) 584,000
(5) 58,400

24. Find the mean population of the 100 largest U.S. cities mentioned in the last problem.

(1) 5,840
(2) 58,400
(3) 584,000
(4) 5,840,000
(5) 58,400,000

Answers are on page **134.**

Chapter 4

Fractions

GED Mathematics pp. 103–136
Complete GED pp. 747–774

Basic Skills

Directions: Use the following list of words to fill in the blanks for problems 1–10.

numerator	denominator	common denominators
proper	improper	mixed number
reducing	reciprocal	raising to higher terms
inverse	canceling	

1. The top number in a fraction is called the _____.

2. The bottom number in a fraction is called the _____.

3. A fraction that is greater than or equal to 1 is called an _____ fraction.

4. A fraction whose numerator is less than the denominator is called a _____ fraction.

5. The number $5\frac{1}{2}$ is an example of a _____.

6. To change a fraction to an equivalent fraction with a larger denominator is called _____.

7. To multiply the fractions $\frac{3}{5} \times \frac{7}{12}$, you can first divide both 3 and 12 by 3. This operation is called _____.

8. To express the fraction $\frac{8}{10}$ in simpler terms, you can divide both 8 and 10 by 2. This operation is called _____.

9. For the fractions $\frac{5}{6}$ and $\frac{1}{4}$, both denominators divide evenly into 12, 24, and 36. Therefore, 12, 24, and 36 are called _____ of $\frac{5}{6}$ and $\frac{1}{4}$.

10. To divide 12 by $\frac{2}{3}$, you can multiply 12 by $\frac{3}{2}$. Therefore, $\frac{3}{2}$ is called the _____ or the _____ of $\frac{2}{3}$.

Solve each problem.

11. Which fractions in this list are equal to $\frac{1}{2}$? $\quad \frac{5}{8} \quad \frac{7}{14} \quad \frac{11}{22} \quad \frac{1}{3} \quad \frac{13}{26}$

12. Which fractions in this list are greater than $\frac{1}{2}$? $\quad \frac{7}{9} \quad \frac{2}{5} \quad \frac{4}{7} \quad \frac{8}{13} \quad \frac{9}{18}$

13. Which fractions in this list are less than $\frac{1}{2}$? $\quad \frac{5}{12} \quad \frac{7}{20} \quad \frac{8}{16} \quad \frac{11}{20} \quad \frac{7}{24}$

14. Reduce each fraction to lowest terms. $\quad \frac{8}{10} \quad \frac{6}{36} \quad \frac{35}{40} \quad \frac{20}{300} \quad \frac{18}{100}$

15. Raise $\frac{4}{5}$ to an equivalent fraction with a denominator of 30.

16. Change $4\frac{2}{3}$ to an improper fraction.

17. Change 0.035 to a fraction and reduce.

18. Express $\frac{5}{12}$ as a decimal rounded to the nearest thousandth.

19. For the problem $5\frac{1}{2} + 6\frac{3}{8} + 2\frac{3}{4}$, round each number to the nearest whole number. Then add the rounded numbers.

20. Find the exact answer to the last problem.

21. For the problem $8\frac{1}{3} - 2\frac{3}{4}$, round each number to the nearest whole number. Then subtract the rounded numbers.

22. Find the exact answer to the last problem.

23. Find $\frac{2}{3}$ of 45.

24. For the problem $1\frac{2}{3} \times 2\frac{1}{4}$, round each number to the nearest whole number. Then find the product of the rounded numbers.

25. Find the exact answer to the last problem.

26. What is $5\frac{1}{3} \div 1\frac{1}{3}$?

27. Evaluate $\left(\frac{3}{5}\right)^2$.

28. What is $\sqrt{\frac{25}{36}}$?

29. Write 0.00038 in scientific notation.

30. Express 2.6×10^{-5} as a decimal.

Answers are on page 135.

GED PRACTICE

PART I

Directions: You may use a calculator to solve the following problems. For problems 1–3, mark each answer on the corresponding number grid.

1. From a 5-foot board, Howard cut a piece $4\frac{1}{4}$ feet long. What was the length, in feet, of the remaining piece?

2. Together, Mr. and Mrs. Vega take home $3000 a month. Each month they put $200 into a savings account. What fraction of their take-home income do they save?

3. Altogether, 384 students are registered for evening classes at Central County High School. Of these students, 256 have full-time jobs. What fraction of the students in evening classes have full-time jobs?

Choose the correct answer to each problem.

4. Assuming no waste, how many strips, each $3\frac{1}{2}$ inches wide, can be cut from a board that is 21 inches wide?

(1) 2
(2) 4
(3) 5
(4) 6
(5) 7

5. Marcia paid $\frac{1}{10}$ of the asking price of $94,000 as a down payment on a previously owned home. How much was the down payment?

(1) $3133
(2) $4700
(3) $5800
(4) $6267
(5) $9400

6. Jane wants to can her cooked apples. Each jar will hold $\frac{3}{4}$ pound of apples. How many jars can she fill from 12 pounds of apples?

    (1) 20
    (2) 18
    (3) 16
    (4) 14
    (5) 12

7. James has paid $\frac{2}{3}$ of his car loan. So far he has paid $3600. How much did he borrow?

    (1) $1200
    (2) $2400
    (3) $3200
    (4) $4800
    (5) $5400

8. In the last problem, how much more does James owe on his car loan?

    (1) $1200
    (2) $1800
    (3) $2400
    (4) $3200
    (5) $3600

9. A pie recipe calls for $\frac{2}{3}$ cup of sugar. How many cups of sugar are required to make five pies?

    (1) $1\frac{2}{3}$
    (2) $2\frac{2}{3}$
    (3) $3\frac{1}{3}$
    (4) $3\frac{2}{3}$
    (5) $4\frac{1}{3}$

10. Carl paid $7.50 for $1\frac{1}{4}$ pounds of lamb chops. What was the price per pound?

    (1) $3
    (2) $4
    (3) $5
    (4) $6
    (5) $7

11. A professional basketball team won 48 games and lost 32. What fraction of the games did the team win?

    (1) $\frac{5}{6}$
    (2) $\frac{3}{4}$
    (3) $\frac{2}{3}$
    (4) $\frac{3}{5}$
    (5) $\frac{2}{5}$

12. Mr. Stone wants to hang 4 shelves, each $15\frac{1}{2}$ inches long, in his bathroom. Assuming no waste, how many inches of shelving does he need?

    (1) 62
    (2) 60
    (3) 58
    (4) 56
    (5) 54

13. A sheet of copy paper is $\frac{1}{250}$ inch thick. Express the thickness in scientific notation.

    (1) 4×10^{-2}
    (2) 4×10^{-3}
    (3) 4×10^{-4}
    (4) 4×10^{-5}
    (5) 4×10^{-6}

PART II

Directions: Solve the following problems without a calculator. For problems 13 and 14, mark each answer on the corresponding number grid.

14. There are 24 students in Alfonso's Spanish class. Of these students, 21 passed their finals with a score of 80 or higher. What fraction of the students passed with a score of 80 or higher?

15. The Richardsons spend $\frac{1}{4}$ of their income on rent, $\frac{1}{3}$ on food, $\frac{1}{6}$ on transportation costs, and another $\frac{1}{6}$ on clothes. Together, these expenses make up what fraction of the Richardsons' budget?

Choose the correct answer to each problem.

16. The Richardsons in the last problem take home $2413 a month. Approximately how much do they spend each month on food?

(1) $300
(2) $450
(3) $650
(4) $800
(5) $925

17. Jake wants to buy a motorbike that costs $5000. So far he has saved $\frac{2}{3}$ of the price of the motorbike. To the nearest 10 dollars, how much has Jake saved?

(1) $4260
(2) $3750
(3) $3330
(4) $2950
(5) $2190

18. From a 2-pound box of sugar, Anne used $1\frac{1}{8}$ pounds to bake cupcakes for her son's school birthday party and then another $\frac{1}{2}$ pound for a cake for the family's party at home. How many pounds of sugar were left in the box?

(1) $\frac{3}{8}$

(2) $\frac{1}{2}$

(3) $\frac{3}{4}$

(4) $\frac{7}{8}$

(5) 1

19. Which of the following best represents a way to approximate the cost of $1\frac{7}{8}$ pounds of chicken that cost $4.99 per pound?

(1) $1 \times \$4 = \$4$
(2) $1 \times \$5 = \$5$
(3) $2 \times \$4 = \$8$
(4) $2 \times \$5 = \$10$
(5) $3 \times \$5 = \$15$

20. Builders often use lumber called 2-by-4s for house construction. The numbers refer to the cross-sectional dimensions of the wood before it is dried and planed. In fact, a 2-by-4 is only $1\frac{1}{2}$ inches by $3\frac{1}{2}$ inches. The illustration shows three 2-by-4s that are nailed together to form a corner column of a house. What is the total depth, in inches, of the three boards?

(1) 12
(2) $10\frac{1}{2}$
(3) 9
(4) $4\frac{1}{2}$
(5) 3

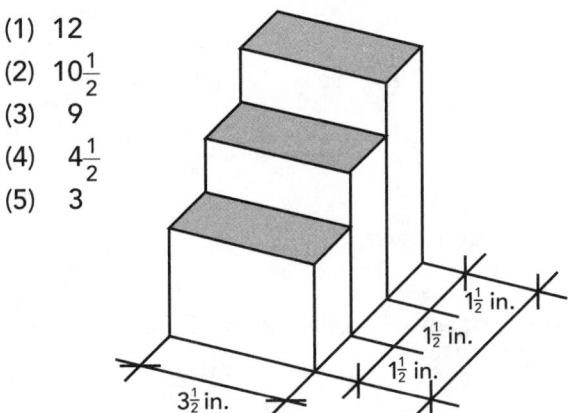

$1\frac{1}{2}$ in.
$1\frac{1}{2}$ in.
$1\frac{1}{2}$ in.
$3\frac{1}{2}$ in.

21. A microbe is 2.6×10^{-5} meter long. Which of the following expresses the length of the microbe in meters?

(1) 2.6
(2) 0.026
(3) 0.0026
(4) 0.00026
(5) 0.000026

22. Oxygen makes up $\frac{13}{20}$ of the weight of the human body, and hydrogen makes up $\frac{1}{10}$ of the weight. Together, these two elements make up what fraction of the total weight of the human body?

(1) $\frac{3}{4}$
(2) $\frac{2}{3}$
(3) $\frac{3}{5}$
(4) $\frac{1}{2}$
(5) $\frac{2}{5}$

23. According to the information in the last problem, a man who weighs 179 pounds is made up of approximately how many pounds of hydrogen?

(1) 12
(2) 15
(3) 18
(4) 21
(5) 24

24. Steve is a builder. He asks his clients to pay $\frac{1}{4}$ of the price of the whole job at the beginning, $\frac{1}{2}$ in six weeks, and the rest when the job is completed. For a new garage, the initial payment was $6500. What is the total price of the job?

(1) $20,000
(2) $26,000
(3) $30,000
(4) $32,000
(5) $36,000

Answers are on page 136.

Chapter 5

Ratio and Proportion

GED Mathematics pp. 137–148
Complete GED pp. 285–292

Basic Skills

Directions: Solve each problem.

For problems 1–3, simplify each ratio.

1. 16:28 =   6:45 =   72:63 =   8:600 =

2. $60 to $100 =   2 to 500 =   75 to 3 =   28 to 56 =

3. $\frac{38}{18}$ = $\frac{1.3}{5.2}$ = $\frac{12,000}{42,000}$ = $\frac{65}{15}$ =

For problems 4 and 5, solve for the unknown in each proportion.

4. $\frac{x}{5} = \frac{7}{9}$ $\frac{12}{x} = \frac{5}{2}$ $\frac{1}{8} = \frac{x}{20}$ $\frac{9}{2} = \frac{15}{x}$

5. $\frac{3}{20} = \frac{x}{120}$ $\frac{8}{5} = \frac{100}{x}$ $\frac{x}{45} = \frac{4}{9}$ $\frac{24}{x} = \frac{6}{7}$

For problems 6–8, choose the correct answer.

6. Which of the following is *not* equal to the ratio 60:80?

    (1) 6:8   (2) 3:4   (3) 3 to 4   (4) $\frac{3}{4}$ (5) $\frac{4}{3}$

7. For the proportion $\frac{9}{12} = \frac{6}{8}$, what are the two cross products?

    (1) 9 × 12 and 6 × 8
    (2) 9 × 6 and 12 × 8
    (3) 9 × 8 and 12 × 6
    (4) 9 × 6 and 8 × 12

8. Which of the following represents the cross products of the proportion 7:5 = 3:x?

    (1) 7 × 5 = 3 × x
    (2) 7 × x = 5 × 3
    (3) 7 × 3 = 5 × x
    (4) 5 × 7 = x × 3

Problems 9–11 refer to the following information.

The lot at a car dealership has 21 new cars and 15 used cars.

9. What is the ratio of new cars to used cars?

10. What is the ratio of used cars to the total number of cars in the lot?

11. What is the ratio of new cars to the total number of cars?

Problems 12 and 13 refer to the following information.

On a math test Oliver got four problems right for every problem
that he got wrong.

12. What was the ratio of the number of problems right to the total
    number of problems?

13. There were 60 problems on the test. How many problems did
    Oliver get right?

Problems 14 and 15 refer to the following information.

For every three new tomato plants that grew in Juanita's garden,
one failed to grow.

14. What is the ratio of the number of tomato plants that grew to the
    number that were planted?

15. Altogether, Juanita planted 24 tomato plants. How many grew?

Answers are on page 137.

Go to **www.GEDMath.com** for additional practice and instruction!

GED PRACTICE

PART I

Directions: You may use a calculator to solve the following problems. For problems 1–3, mark each answer on the corresponding number grid.

Problems 1–3 refer to the following information.

Each month Mr. and Mrs. Sagan pay $620 for their home mortgage. This leaves them with $1860 for other expenses.

1. What is the ratio of the Sagans' mortgage payment to the amount they have each month for other expenses? Express the answer as a reduced fraction.

2. What is the ratio of the Sagans' mortgage payment to their monthly income? Express the answer as a reduced fraction.

3. In dollars, what is the Sagans' yearly income?

Choose the correct answer to each problem.

4. What is the solution for m in $\frac{5}{8} = \frac{12}{m}$?

   (1) $3\frac{1}{3}$

   (2) $7\frac{1}{2}$

   (3) $12\frac{5}{8}$

   (4) $19\frac{1}{5}$

   (5) $21\frac{2}{3}$

5. Which of the following represents the solution for c in $\frac{2}{3} = \frac{c}{11}$?

   (1) $\frac{2 \times 11}{3}$

   (2) $\frac{3 \times 11}{2}$

   (3) $\frac{2 \times 3}{11}$

   (4) $\frac{2}{3 \times 11}$

   (5) $\frac{3}{2 \times 11}$

GED PRACTICE

6. Laura wants to enlarge a photograph to make a poster. The photograph is 4 inches wide and 5 inches long. The long side of the poster will be 30 inches. Find the measurement, in inches, of the short side.

(1) 16

(2) 20

(3) 24

(4) $26\frac{1}{2}$

(5) $37\frac{1}{2}$

7. For a year, the budget of the Central County Senior Services Agency is $360,000. For every $10 in the budget, $1.50 goes to administration. What is the yearly budget for administration at the agency?

(1) $24,000
(2) $32,000
(3) $36,000
(4) $48,000
(5) $54,000

8. To make 2.5 gallons of maple syrup, a farmer needs to collect 100 gallons of sap. How many gallons of sap are needed to make 20 gallons of maple syrup?

(1) 200
(2) 400
(3) 600
(4) 800
(5) 1000

9. To make a certain color of paint, Mavis needs 4 units of yellow paint for every 1 unit of white paint. She estimates that she will need 15 gallons of paint to complete her job. How many gallons of white paint will she need?

(1) 2
(2) 3
(3) 5
(4) 6
(5) 8

10. If three oranges sell for $1.29, what is the price of 8 oranges?

(1) $2.19
(2) $2.33
(3) $2.77
(4) $3.29
(5) $3.44

11. One inch on the scale of a map is equal to 48 miles. How many miles apart are two cities that are $3\frac{1}{4}$ inches apart on the map?

(1) 156
(2) 135
(3) 119
(4) 107
(5) 90

12. Boston is 315 miles from Philadelphia. If the scale on the map is 1 inch = 20 miles, how many inches apart are Boston and Philadelphia?

(1) $10\frac{1}{2}$

(2) $12\frac{1}{3}$

(3) $15\frac{3}{4}$

(4) $18\frac{1}{4}$

(5) $19\frac{1}{2}$

13. Which of the following is *not* equivalent to the ratio 24:32?

(1) 9:12

(2) $\frac{3}{4}$

(3) 0.75

(4) 15:21

(5) 6 ÷ 8

14. Which of the following expresses the simplified form of the ratio $\frac{7}{8}$ to $\frac{5}{6}$?

(1) 10:9

(2) 13:12

(3) 16:15

(4) 19:18

(5) 21:20

PART II

Directions: Solve the following problems without a calculator. For problems 15 and 16, mark each answer on the corresponding number grid.

15. A newspaper printed 10,000 copies. Of these copies, 80 were defective and had to be discarded. What is the ratio of defective copies to the total number printed? Express your answer as a reduced fraction.

16. Solve for n in $\frac{n}{10} = \frac{7}{40}$. Express your answer as a decimal.

Choose the correct answer to each problem.

17. In Buffalo one November, rain was recorded on 9 days; snow was recorded on 6 days; and on another 3 days, a combination of rain, snow, or other precipitation was recorded. What is the ratio of the number of days when some precipitation was recorded to the total number of days in the month?

(1) 1:2

(2) 2:3

(3) 3:4

(4) 3:5

(5) 4:5

18. Phil saves $1 for every $8 that he spends. If Phil takes home $720 a week, how much does he save each week?

(1) $75

(2) $80

(3) $85

(4) $90

(5) $95

GED PRACTICE

19. A 9-foot-tall sapling casts a shadow 2.5 feet long. At the same time, an old pine tree casts a shadow 20 feet long. How many feet tall is the pine tree?

    (1) 54
    (2) 63
    (3) 72
    (4) 81
    (5) 90

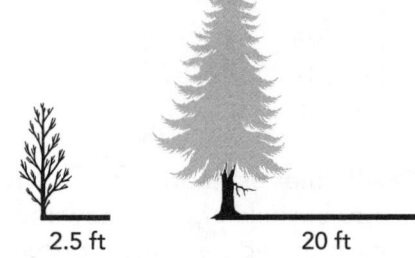

2.5 ft   20 ft

Problems 20–22 refer to the following information.

A polling organization interviewed 600 people about a proposed cement plant in their community. Of the people interviewed, 312 were in favor of the new plant in their community, 193 were against it, and the rest were undecided.

20. How many people were undecided?

    (1) 115
    (2) 105
    (3) 95
    (4) 85
    (5) 75

21. What is the approximate ratio of the number of people who were in favor of the plant to the number who were against it?

    (1) 6:5
    (2) 5:4
    (3) 4:3
    (4) 3:2
    (5) 2:1

22. What was the approximate ratio of the number of people who were undecided to the total number of people who were interviewed?

    (1) 1:2
    (2) 1:3
    (3) 1:4
    (4) 1:5
    (5) 1:6

Problems 23–25 refer to the following information.

One commonly used formula for making concrete is to mix 1 unit of cement to 2 units of sand and 4 units of gravel.

23. What is the ratio of sand to gravel in the mixture?

    (1) 1:2
    (2) 2:3
    (3) 3:4
    (4) 4:5
    (5) 5:6

24. What is the ratio of cement to the combination of sand and gravel?

    (1) 1:6
    (2) 1:5
    (3) 1:4
    (4) 1:3
    (5) 1:2

25. A 1000-pound slab of concrete contains about how many pounds of sand?

    (1) 110
    (2) 190
    (3) 290
    (4) 330
    (5) 390

GED PRACTICE

Choose the correct answer to each problem.

26. Which of the following represents a solution to the proportion 4:5 = x:70?

(1) $x = \dfrac{5}{4 \times 70}$

(2) $x = \dfrac{4}{5 \times 70}$

(3) $x = \dfrac{4 \times 5}{70}$

(4) $x = \dfrac{4 \times 70}{5}$

(5) $x = \dfrac{5 \times 70}{4}$

27. For every $1 that Angie spends in a restaurant, she leaves a tip of 15¢. When Angie took her father out to lunch, the bill came to $29.89. Which of the following is the closest approximation of the tip that she left?

(1) $1.50
(2) $2.50
(3) $3.75
(4) $4.50
(5) $6.00

28. A baseball team won 3 games for every 2 that they lost. In a season when the team played 160 games, how many games did they win?

(1) 74
(2) 85
(3) 96
(4) 101
(5) 108

29. A farmer estimates that 1 acre will produce 120 bushels of corn. How many acres of corn should he plant in order to yield 3000 bushels of corn?

(1) 15
(2) 25
(3) 35
(4) 40
(5) 50

Answers are on page 137.

Chapter 6

Percent

GED Mathematics pp. 149–182
Complete GED pp. 793–808

Basic Skills

Directions: Write each percent as a fraction in lowest terms.

1. 25% =   50% =   75% =

2. 20% =   40% =   60% =   80% =

3. $33\frac{1}{3}\%$ = $66\frac{2}{3}\%$ =

4. $12\frac{1}{2}\%$ = $37\frac{1}{2}\%$ = $62\frac{1}{2}\%$ = $87\frac{1}{2}\%$ =

Write each percent as a decimal.

5. 1% =   10% =   100% =   1000% =

6. 25% =   50% =   75% =

7. 20% =   40% =   60% =   80% =

8. 8% =   4.5% =   85% =   110% =

9. Which of the following is *not* equal to 50%? $\frac{1}{2}$ 0.5 $\frac{1}{5}$ $\frac{3}{6}$

10. Which of the following is *not* equal to 100%?   1   2 $\frac{2}{2}$ 1.0

Use the statement "25% of 32 is 8" to answer problems 11–13.

11. The part is _____.

12. The percent is _____.

13. The whole is _____.

55

Use the statement "35 is 1% of 3500" to answer problems 14–16.

14. The part is _____.

15. The percent is _____.

16. The whole is _____.

For problems 17–22, first tell whether you are looking for the *part,* the *percent,* or the *whole.* Then solve each problem.

17. 50% of 66 = $33\frac{1}{3}$% of 120 =   80% of 35 =

18. 10% of 325 =   40% of 90 =   6.5% of 200 =

19. 8 is what % of 32?   What % of 38 is 19?

20. 10 is what % of 200?   What % of 36 is 12?

21. 16 is 80% of what number?   50% of what number is 17?

22. 40 is $33\frac{1}{3}$% of what number?   60% of what number is 150?

Solve the following problems.

23. The Rogers family's rent went from $450 a month last year to $477 a month this year. By what percent did their rent increase?

24. On the opening day of a crafts fair, 1200 people bought admissions tickets. On the second day, there was heavy rain, and only 900 people bought tickets. By what percent did the attendance drop the second day?

25. Calculate the interest on $1500 at 14% annual interest for 4 months.

Answers are on page 139.

GED PRACTICE

PART I

Directions: You may use a calculator to solve the following problems. For problems 1–3, mark each answer on the corresponding number grid.

1. Change 15% to a common fraction and reduce to lowest terms.

2. What is 8.7% of 40?

3. 9.3 is 60% of what number?

Choose the correct answer to each problem.

4. The price of a gallon of heating oil rose from $1.60 a gallon to $1.92. By what percent did the price increase?

(1)   5%
(2) 10%
(3) 15%
(4) 20%
(5) 25%

5. In 1990 there were 40 members in the County Rowing Club. In 2000 the club had 70 members. By what percent did the membership increase?

(1) 55%
(2) 60%
(3) 65%
(4) 70%
(5) 75%

6. A shirt is on sale for $29.95. What will the sales tax on the shirt be if the sales tax rate is $7\frac{1}{2}$%?

(1) $1.99
(2) $2.10
(3) $2.25
(4) $2.99
(5) $3.10

7. The Parent-Teacher Organization sent out requests for donations to buy new athletic equipment. Within one week, 210 people had sent in their donations. This represents 15% of the total requests that were mailed. How many requests did the organization send out?

   (1) 2100
   (2) 1400
   (3) 1050
   (4) 640
   (5) 315

8. Of the 30 students in Bob's exercise class, 80% drive to class. The rest walk or ride bicycles. How many of the students do not drive to the class?

   (1) 6
   (2) 8
   (3) 12
   (4) 15
   (5) 20

9. Kyle bought a boat for $4500. Five years later he sold it for $3600. What percent of the purchase price did Kyle lose?

   (1) 5%
   (2) 9%
   (3) 11%
   (4) 15%
   (5) 20%

10. Phil and Barbara's house has a floor area of 1600 square feet. Phil put on an addition with a floor area of 600 square feet. By what percent does the addition increase the area of the house?

    (1) 30%
    (2) 50%
    (3) $37\frac{1}{2}$%
    (4) 60%
    (5) $62\frac{1}{2}$%

11. Adrienne had to pay $5.40 sales tax on a pair of ski boots. The sales tax rate in her state is 4.5%. What was the price of the boots?

    (1) $120
    (2) $100
    (3) $ 90
    (4) $ 85
    (5) $ 45

12. What will the simple interest be on $2500 at $8\frac{1}{2}$% annual interest for 6 months?

    (1) $212.50
    (2) $158.00
    (3) $127.50
    (4) $106.25
    (5) $ 70.80

Problems 13 and 14 refer to the following information.

A store offered a computer for $998. The sales tax in the state where the store is located is 6%. On Labor Day the store offered 10% off all electronic equipment.

13. What is the regular price of the computer, including sales tax?

    (1) $ 938.12
    (2) $ 998.06
    (3) $1004.00
    (4) $1057.88
    (5) $1097.80

14. What is the Labor Day sale price of the computer, not including tax?

    (1) $848.30
    (2) $898.20
    (3) $938.12
    (4) $948.10
    (5) $988.00

15. A hardware store offered a lawn mower for $180 during the summer. On Labor Day they offered garden equipment at 10% off the regular price, but later in September they offered an additional 5% off the Labor Day sale price for all garden equipment. Find the late September sale price of the lawn mower.

(1) $149.10
(2) $152.00
(3) $153.90
(4) $159.10
(5) $165.00

PART II

Directions: Solve the following problems without a calculator. For problems 16 and 17, mark each answer on the corresponding number grid.

16. Change 175% to a decimal.

17. Find 2% of 140. Express your answer as a decimal.

Choose the correct answer to each problem.

18. Mr. Sanchez weighed 220 pounds. He went on a diet and lost 20% of his weight. Find his new weight in pounds.

(1) 200
(2) 180
(3) 176
(4) 160
(5) 155

19. An outdoor barbecue is on sale for $139. Which expression represents the price of the barbecue, including a 6% sales tax?

(1) $0.6 \times \$139$
(2) $0.06 \times \$139$
(3) $1.6 \times \$139$
(4) $1.06 \times \$139$
(5) $0.16 \times \$139$

20. Bonnie borrowed $800 from her sister. So far she has paid back $480. Which of the following does *not* represent the part of the loan Bonnie has paid back?

    (1) $\frac{480}{800}$

    (2) 60%

    (3) 0.6

    (4) $\frac{3}{5}$

    (5) $\frac{48}{100}$

21. Which of the following represents one month's interest on an outstanding credit card debt of $2700 if the annual interest rate is 18%?

    (1) $\frac{\$2700 \times 0.18}{12}$

    (2) $\frac{12 \times 0.18}{\$2700}$

    (3) $\frac{\$2700 \times 12}{0.18}$

    (4) $\frac{\$2700 \times 1.8}{12}$

    (5) $\frac{\$2700 \times 18}{12}$

22. On July 4th a furniture store is selling everything for 10% off the regular price. Which expression represents the sale price of a garden chair that regularly sold for $16.95?

    (1) $0.1 \times \$16.95$
    (2) $1.1 \times \$16.95$
    (3) $0.9 \times \$16.95$
    (4) $0.8 \times \$16.95$
    (5) $0.01 \times \$16.95$

23. An advertisement for new high-speed Internet access claims that pages will load up to 5000% faster. Which of the following is the same as 5000% faster?

    (1) 0.5 times faster
    (2) 5 times faster
    (3) 50 times faster
    (4) 500 times faster
    (5) 5000 times faster

24. Membership in a concerned citizens organization went from 60 in 1999 to 115 in 2001. To calculate the percent of increase in membership, multiply 100% by which of the following expressions?

    (1) $\frac{60 - 115}{115}$

    (2) $\frac{115 - 60}{60}$

    (3) $\frac{115 - 60}{115}$

    (4) $\frac{60}{115}$

    (5) $\frac{115}{60}$

25. According to the Department of Transportation, approximately 15,000 U.S. flights were delayed from 1 to 2 hours in 1995. In 2000 that number increased by about 150%. Approximately how many flights in the U.S. were delayed from 1 to 2 hours in 2000?

    (1) 20,000
    (2) 22,500
    (3) 27,500
    (4) 32,500
    (5) 37,500

26. A technology stock sold for $80 a share. Then, after the company announced that they would fail to meet sales expectations, the price of a share dropped by 60%. What was the price of a share after the announcement?

    (1) $74
    (2) $54
    (3) $48
    (4) $32
    (5) $28

27. Mr. and Mrs. Gonzalez bought their house in 1971 for $25,000. In order to move into a retirement home, they sold the house in 2001 for $200,000. By what percent did the price of the house increase from 1971 to 2001?

    (1) 700%
    (2) 500%
    (3) 350%
    (4) 140%
    (5) 70%

28. Which of the following represents the simple interest on $3000 at 6.5% annual interest for 8 months?

    (1) $3000 \times 0.65 \times 8$
    (2) $3000 \times 0.065 \times \frac{2}{3}$
    (3) $3000 \times 0.65 \times \frac{3}{2}$
    (4) $3000 \times 0.065 \times 8$
    (5) $3000 \times 6.5 \times \frac{2}{3}$

29. In a recent year, the total value of athletic shoes sold in the U.S. was about $15 billion. Of this amount, 13% was for children from 4 to 12 years old. What was the approximate value of athletic shoes purchased for 4- to 12-year-old children?

    (1) $0.5 billion
    (2) $1 billion
    (3) $1.5 billion
    (4) $2 billion
    (5) $2.5 billion

30. The population of Capital County is 492,385. Experts estimate that 10% of the population of the county immigrated from other countries. About how many people in the county immigrated from other countries?

    (1) 75,000
    (2) 60,000
    (3) 50,000
    (4) 40,000
    (5) 35,000

Answers are on page 139.

 Go to **www.GEDMath.com** for additional practice and instruction!

Chapter 7

Measurement

GED Mathematics pp. 183–196
Complete GED pp. 873–892

Basic Skills

Directions: For problems 1–4, fill in each blank with the correct equivalent of each customary unit of measure. Then check and correct your answers before you continue.

1. Measures of Length

   1 foot (ft)   = _____ inches (in.)

   1 yard (yd)   = _____ inches

   1 yard   = _____ feet

   1 mile (mi)   = _____ feet

   1 mile   = _____ yards

2. Measures of Weight

   1 pound (lb) = _____ ounces (oz)

   1 ton (T)   = _____ pounds

3. Liquid Measures

   1 pint (pt)   = _____ ounces

   1 cup   = _____ ounces

   1 pint   = _____ cups

   1 quart (qt) = _____ pints

   1 gallon (gal) = _____ quarts

4. Measures of Time

   1 minute (min) = _____ seconds (sec)

   1 hour (hr)   = _____ minutes

   1 day   = _____ hours

   1 week (wk)   = _____ days

   1 year (yr)   = _____ days

For problems 5–8, change each unit to the larger unit indicated. Express each answer as a fraction in lowest terms.

5. 1200 pounds = _____ ton   6 hours = _____ day

6. 6 inches = _____ foot   12 ounces = _____ pound

7. 45 minutes = _____ hour   1 quart = _____ gallon

8. 21 inches = _____ yard   4 inches = _____ foot

For problems 9–11, change each unit to the smaller unit indicated.

9. 2 pounds = _____ ounces   6 feet = _____ inches

10. 3 minutes = _____ seconds   5 yards = _____ feet

11. 10 tons = _____ pounds   3 days = _____ hours

For problems 12–14, fill in each blank with the correct equivalent of each metric unit of measure. Then check and correct your answers before you continue.

12. Measures of Length

    1 meter (m)   = _____ millimeters (mm)

    1 meter   = _____ centimeters (cm)

    1 kilometer (km)   = _____ meters

    1 decimeter (dm)   = _____ meter

13. Measures of Weight

    1 gram (g)   = _____ milligrams (mg)

    1 kilogram (kg)   = _____ grams

14. Liquid Measures

    1 liter (L)   = _____ milliliters (mL)

    1 deciliter (dL)   = _____ liter

For problems 15–18, change each metric measurement to the unit indicated.

15. 3.15 kilograms = _____ grams   2 kilometers = _____ meters

16. 4 meters = _____ centimeters   1.5 liters = _____ milliliters

17. 60 centimeters = _____ meter   850 grams = _____ kilogram

18. 250 meters = _____ kilometer   135 milliliters = _____ liter

Solve the following problems.

19. Change 20 ounces to pounds. Express your answer as a decimal (a whole number and a decimal).

20. Change 21 inches to feet. Express your answer as a mixed number (a whole number and a fraction).

21. Change 2500 pounds to tons and pounds.

22. Change 90 minutes to hours. Express your answer as a decimal.

23. Change 10 quarts to gallons. Express your answer as a mixed number.

24. Change 5680 feet to miles and feet.

25. For each letter on the $4\frac{1}{2}$-inch ruler below, tell the distance, in inches, from 0.

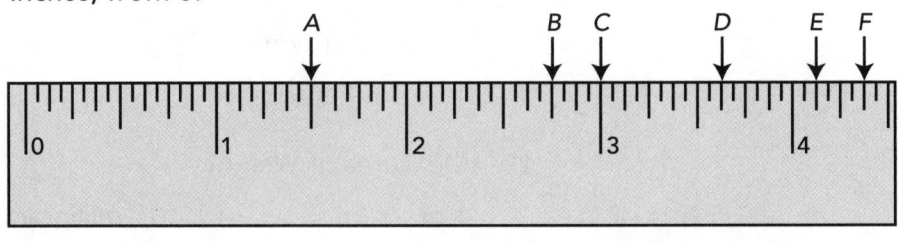

A =   B =   C =   D =   E =   F =

26. For each letter on the 11-centimeter ruler below, tell the distance, in centimeters, from 0.

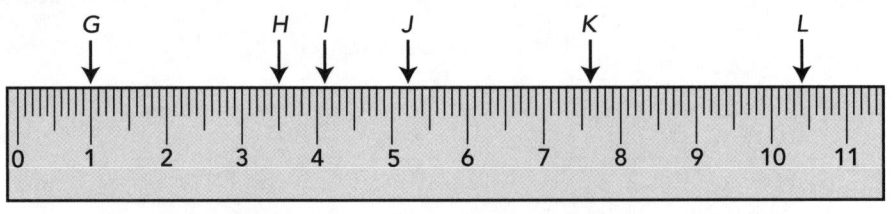

G =   H =   I =   J =   K =   L =

GED PRACTICE

PART I

Directions: You may use a calculator to solve the following problems. For problems 1–3, mark each answer on the corresponding number grid.

1. Paula used 6 ounces of sugar from a 2-pound bag. What fraction of the sugar in the bag did she use?

2. What is the mean weight of three parcels that weigh 0.6 kilogram, 1.41 kilograms, and 1.8 kilograms?

3. Normal body temperature is 98.6° Fahrenheit. When he had the flu, Mack's temperature reached 103.5°F. How many degrees above normal was his temperature?

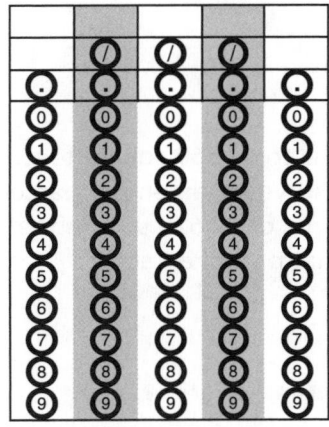

Choose the correct answer to each problem.

4. The formula $C = \frac{5}{9}(F - 32)$ converts Fahrenheit temperature (F) to Celsius temperature (C). What is the Celsius temperature that corresponds to a healthy body temperature of 98.6° Fahrenheit?

   (1) 31°
   (2) 33°
   (3) 35°
   (4) 37°
   (5) 39°

5. It takes $\frac{1}{10}$ of a second for a voltmeter to rise one volt. Approximately how many seconds will it take the voltmeter to reach the reading shown below?

   (1) 75.0
   (2) 70.0
   (3) 7.5
   (4) 0.75
   (5) 0.0075

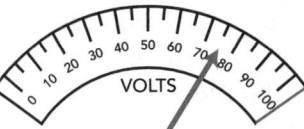

6. At $5.89 a pound, what is the price of a can of coffee that weighs 8 ounces?

   (1) $3.89
   (2) $3.11
   (3) $2.95
   (4) $2.89
   (5) $2.68

7. One acre is equal to 43,560 square feet. According to a surveyor, an empty parcel of land has an area of 32,670 square feet. The parcel is what part of an acre?

   (1) 0.25
   (2) 0.3
   (3) 0.5
   (4) 0.65
   (5) 0.75

8. What is the distance, in centimeters, from point A to point B on the 5-centimeter ruler below?

   (1) 1.7
   (2) 2.3
   (3) 2.7
   (4) 3.3
   (5) 3.7

9. Roast beef costs $3.69 a pound. Find the cost of 1 pound 12 ounces of roast beef.

   (1) $6.46
   (2) $5.54
   (3) $4.81
   (4) $4.43
   (5) $3.81

10. Meg is making costumes for her daughter's school play. Each costume requires 2 yards 9 inches of material. How many costumes can she make from 20 yards of material?

    (1) 8
    (2) 9
    (3) 10
    (4) 11
    (5) 12

Problems 11 and 12 refer to the following information.

The Internal Revenue Service published the following list of the estimated time a taxpayer would spend completing a long form and three accompanying schedules.

Record keeping	7 hours 52 minutes
Learning about the forms	7 hours 16 minutes
Preparing the forms	10 hours 5 minutes
Assembling and sending	1 hour 49 minutes

11. According to the IRS estimate, which of the following represents the total time a taxpayer needs to spend completing a long form and three schedules?

    (1) 19 hr 42 min
    (2) 21 hr 12 min
    (3) 23 hr 32 min
    (4) 25 hr 2 min
    (5) 27 hr 2 min

12. Jack had to complete a long form and three schedules. He kept a careful record of his time and calculated that he had spent a total of exactly 24 hours working on the tax forms. The time Jack spent was what fraction of the estimated time published by the IRS?

    (1) $\frac{9}{10}$

    (2) $\frac{8}{9}$

    (3) $\frac{7}{8}$

    (4) $\frac{5}{6}$

    (5) $\frac{3}{4}$

13. How many miles can Bill drive in 2 hours
15 minutes if he maintains an average
speed of 64 mph?

(1) 144
(2) 138
(3) 128
(4) 114
(5) 98

14. One pound is approximately 0.453 kilogram.
Betty weighs 127 pounds. What is her
weight to the nearest tenth of a kilogram?

(1) 25.4
(2) 32.6
(3) 45.3
(4) 57.5
(5) 63.5

15. Driving at an average speed of 45 mph,
Linda will need how many minutes to drive
to a town that is 24 miles away?

(1) 24
(2) 28
(3) 32
(4) 36
(5) 40

16. The train trip from Buffalo to New York City
is scheduled to take 7 hours 28 minutes.
Because of track work, the train was late by
1 hour 20 minutes. The train left Buffalo on
schedule at 8:55 A.M. At what time did it
arrive in New York City?

(1) 4:23 P.M.
(2) 4:53 P.M.
(3) 5:23 P.M.
(4) 5:43 P.M.
(5) 6:03 P.M.

PART II

Directions: Solve the following problems
without a calculator. For problems 16 and 17,
mark each answer on the corresponding number
grid.

17. Change 245 centimeters to meters. Express
your answer as a decimal.

18. Ten ounces are what fraction of a pound?

Choose the correct answer to each problem.

19. The formula $F = \frac{9}{5}C + 32$ converts Celsius temperature to Fahrenheit temperature. A temperature of 40° Celsius in Rio de Janeiro corresponds to what Fahrenheit temperature?

- (1) 78°
- (2) 84°
- (3) 94°
- (4) 104°
- (5) 108°

20. What is the distance, in inches, between point C and point D on the 2-inch ruler below?

- (1) $\frac{7}{16}$
- (2) $\frac{9}{16}$
- (3) $\frac{11}{16}$
- (4) $1\frac{3}{16}$
- (5) $1\frac{5}{16}$

21. Which of the following represents the weight, in pounds, of three cans of tuna fish, each weighing 6 ounces?

- (1) $\frac{3 \times 16}{6}$
- (2) $\frac{3 \times 6}{16}$
- (3) $\frac{6 \times 16}{3}$
- (4) $\frac{16}{3 \times 6}$
- (5) $\frac{6}{3 \times 16}$

22. The kilogram scales show the weights of two crates. How many kilograms heavier is crate 1 than crate 2?

- (1) 25
- (2) 28
- (3) 35
- (4) 38
- (5) 42

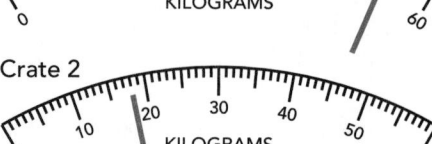

23. Sam has to drive from Jacksonville to Ft. Lauderdale on Highway 1. The distance between the two cities is 324 miles. Sam stopped for a break in West Palm Beach, which is 281 miles from Jacksonville. Approximately what fraction of the total drive had Sam completed when he took the break?

- (1) $\frac{1}{2}$
- (2) $\frac{2}{3}$
- (3) $\frac{3}{4}$
- (4) $\frac{7}{8}$
- (5) $\frac{9}{10}$

24. What is the reading on the Fahrenheit thermometer pictured below?

- (1) 98.9°
- (2) 99.4°
- (3) 99.9°
- (4) 100.1°
- (5) 101.1°

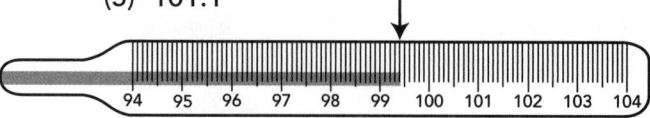

25. Carmen drove for 2 hours at 55 mph and then for another $1\frac{1}{2}$ hours at 12 mph. Which expression represents her average speed for the whole trip?

(1) $\dfrac{55 + 12}{3.5}$

(2) $\dfrac{55 \times 2 + 12 \times 1.5}{2}$

(3) $\dfrac{55 \times 2 + 12 \times 1.5}{3.5}$

(4) $\dfrac{55 \times 3.5 + 12 \times 1.5}{1.5}$

(5) $\dfrac{12 \times 2 + 55 \times 1.5}{3.5}$

26. What is the reading, in amps, on the meter shown below?

(1) 7
(2) 13
(3) 17
(4) 23
(5) 27

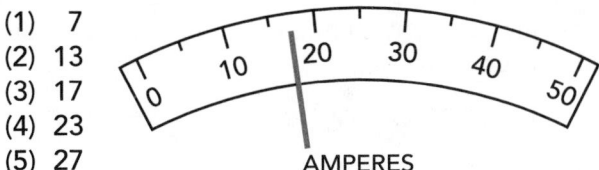

AMPERES

27. The illustration below shows a 1-pint measuring cup. The shaded part represents cooking oil. Which of the following does *not* represent the amount of cooking oil in the measuring cup?

(1) 14 ounces

(2) $1\frac{3}{4}$ cups

(3) $\frac{7}{8}$ pint

(4) $\frac{1}{2}$ quart

(5) 1 cup 6 ounces

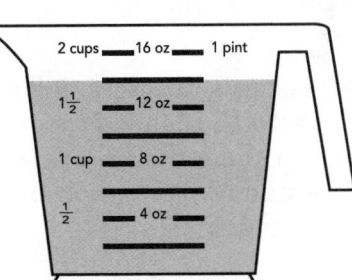

28. The two scales show Mark's weight before and after his diet. What percent of Mark's original weight did he lose?

(1) 5%
(2) 10%
(3) 12.5%
(4) 15%
(5) 20%

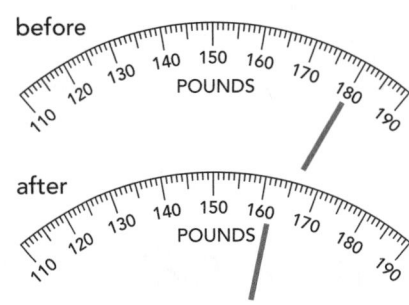

29. The illustration below shows five dials from an electric meter. The leftmost dial represents the ten-thousands place. The second dial represents thousands. The third represents hundreds, and so on. Notice that the numbers alternate from clockwise to counterclockwise. When an arrow appears between two numbers, read the lower number. What is the kilowatt-hour reading of the dials?

KILOWATT HOURS

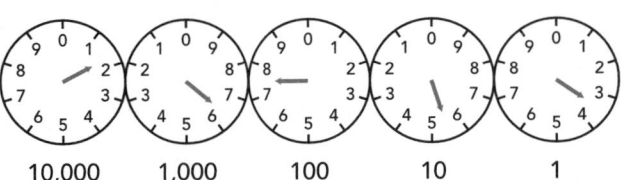

10,000   1,000   100   10   1

(1) 26,853
(2) 26,753
(3) 17,754
(4) 17,853
(5) 16,753

Answers are on page 142.

Chapter 8

Data Analysis, Statistics, and Probability

GED Mathematics pp. 197–222
Complete GED pp. 785–792, 809–834

Basic Skills

Directions: Four circle graphs are pictured below. Each graph is the same size but is divided differently. Following the graphs are four situations that can be represented on circle graphs. For problems 1–4, choose the circle graph that best represents the data described in each situation.

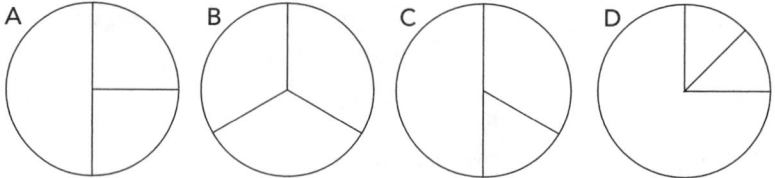

1. An after-school tutorial program gets 75% of its funding from the state. The remaining 25% comes in equal parts from fund-raising events and corporate donors. Which graph best represents the sources of the program's funding?

2. Three partners started a business. Bill invested $24,000, and Steve and Tim each invested $12,000. Now that the business is making a profit, they want to share their profit according to the amount each partner invested. Which graph best represents the profit division for the partnership?

3. For every dollar that the Kim family makes, $0.30 goes for rent, and $0.20 goes for food. The rest is for all of their other expenses. Which graph best represents the Kim family's budget?

4. The Best Bread Baking Company employs workers in three shifts. Forty-five people work from 8:00 in the morning until 4:00 in the afternoon, 45 work from 4:00 in the afternoon until midnight, and 45 work from midnight until 8:00 in the morning. Which graph best represents the number of employees in each shift?

Problems 5–9 refer to the bar graph below.

5. What is the unit of measure of the vertical axis?

   (1) dollars   (2) years
   (3) percent   (4) reservations

PERCENTAGE OF AIR TRAVEL
RESERVATIONS MADE ONLINE

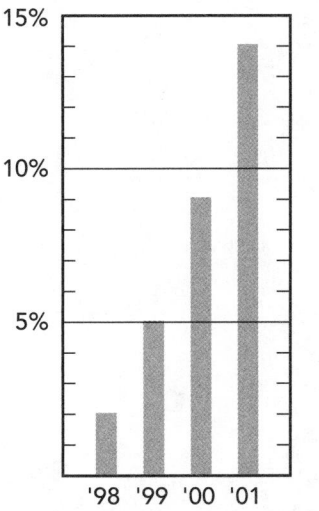

Source: *The New York Times*

6. What is the unit of measure of the horizontal axis?

   (1) dollars   (2) years
   (3) percent   (4) reservations

7. What percent of air travel reservations were made online in 1998?

8. In what year were 9% of air travel reservations made online?

9. For the years shown on the graph, which of the following best describes the trend in making air travel reservations?

   (1) The number of air travel reservations made by professional travel agents has increased steadily.
   (2) The percentage of air travel reservations made online has remained about the same.
   (3) The percentage of air travel reservations made online has increased steadily.
   (4) The number of air travel reservations has dropped in recent years.

Problems 10–12 refer to the list below which tells the names and ages of all the cousins in the Robertson family.

Ann 14	Joe 12	Ryan 24	Tom 17
Jack 22	Megan 23	Sam 14	

10. What is the median age of the Robertson cousins?

11. What is the mean age of the Robertson cousins?

12. What is the mode (the age that occurs most frequently) of the Robertson cousins' ages?

Problems 13–17 refer to the line graph below.

13. At what hour was the temperature the lowest?

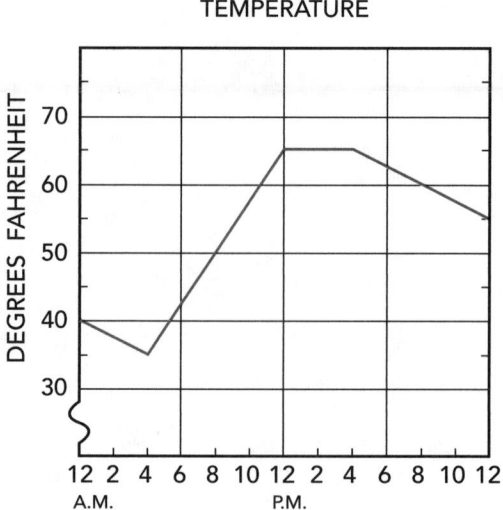

14. What was the lowest temperature for the period shown on the graph?

15. What was the highest temperature for the period shown on the graph?

16. What was the difference between the first temperature and the last temperature for the period shown on the graph?

17. For which of the following time periods did the temperature remain the same?

 (1) midnight to 4 A.M.
 (2) 8 A.M. to noon
 (3) noon to 4 P.M.
 (4) 8 P.M. to midnight

Five line graphs are pictured below. On each graph the horizontal axis is measured in time, but the vertical axes are not labeled. Following the graphs are five situations that can be represented on line graphs. For problems 18–22, choose the line graph that best represents the data described in each situation.

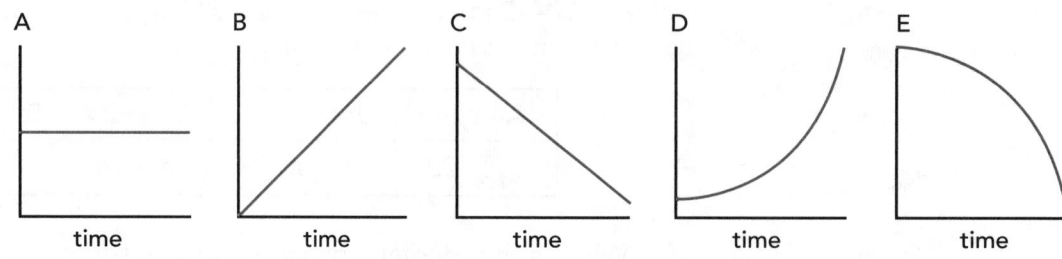

18. The cost of a gallon of gasoline dropped steadily over a 5-week period. Which graph best represents a steady drop?

19. The number of households with Internet access rose at an increasingly faster rate over an 8-year period. Which graph best represents an increasingly rapid rise?

20. A stock that sold for $24 a share at the beginning of the month remained at the same price for the entire month. Which graph best represents an unchanging price?

PART I

Directions: You may use a calculator to solve the following problems. For problems 1–3, mark each answer on the corresponding number grid.

Problems 1–3 refer to the table below showing gasoline mileage in 2000 and goals for gasoline mileage in 2008.

Gasoline Consumption in Average Miles per Gallon		
	2000	2008
Europe	33.0	41.0
Japan	30.3	35.3
U.S.	24.0	25.6

Source: Argonne National Laboratory

1. Japan hopes to have average gas mileage of how many miles per gallon in 2008?

2. For 2008, the goal for gas mileage in Europe is how many more miles per gallon than the goal for the U.S. in that year?

3. The goal for gas mileage in 2008 in Europe is what percent higher than the average 2000 gas mileage in Europe? Round your answer to the nearest tenth percent.

21. Over a 10-year period, the sale of 45-rpm records dropped at an increasingly rapid rate. Which graph best represents an increasingly rapid decline?

22. The population of an early settlement in Kansas rose steadily over a 75-year period. Which graph best represents a steady increase?

Problems 23–25 refer to the following table showing the median income of men and women in a recent year.

Median Weekly Income		
	men	women
Total work force	$618	$473
Registered nurses	791	747
Noncollege teachers	768	659

Source: Bureau of Labor Statistics

23. The median weekly income for men working as noncollege teachers is how much more than for women in the same job?

24. Based on a 52-week year, what is the difference between the median yearly income for men and women in the total work force?

25. Men working as registered nurses make a median income that is what percent greater than the median income of men in the total work force? Round your answer to the nearest percent.

Problems 26 and 27 refer to the information below.

Margaret took a plastic bag of empty cans to a store that had a machine for recycling cans. In her plastic bag were 7 cola cans, 8 orange drink cans, 4 grape soda cans, and 5 sparkling water cans.

26. What is the probability that the first can she pulls out of the bag will be an orange drink can?

27. In fact, the first two cans she took out of the bag were both sparkling water cans. What is the probability that the next can she takes from the bag will be a grape soda can?

Choose the correct answer to each problem. Problems 4–6 refer to the following information.

In a recent year, Wisconsin produced 27% of the cheese in the U.S., California produced 18%, and New York produced 9%.

4. The amount of cheese produced in California was what percent of the amount produced in Wisconsin?

   (1) 75%
   (2) $66\frac{2}{3}\%$
   (3) 50%
   (4) $33\frac{1}{3}\%$
   (5) 25%

5. What percent of the cheese produced in the U.S. was produced in states other than Wisconsin, California, and New York?

   (1) 46%
   (2) 54%
   (3) 56%
   (4) 63%
   (5) 73%

6. A circle contains 360°. The Department of Agriculture wants to represent the cheese production in the U.S. on a circle graph. The pie-shaped piece representing Wisconsin will contain how many degrees?

   (1) 27°
   (2) 54°
   (3) 64.8°
   (4) 97.2°
   (5) 162°

Problems 7–9 refer to the table below.

Students in Bob's Chess Class	
age range	no. of students
50 and over	4
40–49	6
30–39	8
20–29	5
under 20	2

7. How many students in Bob's class are age 40 or older?

   (1) 6
   (2) 8
   (3) 10
   (4) 12
   (5) 18

8. What percent of the students in Bob's class are younger than 30?

   (1) 20%
   (2) 28%
   (3) 35%
   (4) 60%
   (5) 65%

9. Which age range represents the mode (the category with the most students)?

   (1) 50 and over
   (2) 40–49
   (3) 30–39
   (4) 20–29
   (5) under 20

Problems 10 and 11 refer to the table below which describes the cars that are for sale at Carl's on the first day of May.

Carl's Cars	
large	4
midsize	26
small	12

10. What is the probability that the first car sold in May will be a midsize car?

(1) $\frac{8}{21}$

(2) $\frac{13}{21}$

(3) $\frac{1}{26}$

(4) $\frac{26}{1}$

(5) $\frac{21}{13}$

11. In fact, the first two cars sold off Carl's lot in May were small cars. What is the probability that the next car sold will be a large car?

(1) $\frac{1}{10}$

(2) $\frac{1}{8}$

(3) $\frac{1}{6}$

(4) $\frac{1}{4}$

(5) $\frac{1}{2}$

Problems 12–14 refer to the information below. The table comes from a state income tax form. This section of the form is to help a head of household calculate estimated tax.

If line 5 is:		
over	but not over	the tax is:
$ 0	$11,000	4% of line 5
11,000	15,000	$444 plus 4.5% of the excess over $11,000
15,000	17,000	$620 plus 5.25% of the excess over $15,000
17,000	30,000	$725 plus 5.9% of the excess over $17,000

12. Calculate the tax if the amount on line 5 is $8,000.

(1) $240
(2) $320
(3) $360
(4) $400
(5) $440

13. Calculate the tax if the amount on line 5 is $12,800.

(1) $444
(2) $450
(3) $489
(4) $525
(5) $810

14. Calculate the tax if the amount on line 5 is $25,000.

(1) $ 472
(2) $ 727
(3) $1197
(4) $1315
(5) $1475

15. The illustration shows a triangular hotplate made of white and blue tiles. What is the probability of a fly landing on one of the white tiles?

(1) $\frac{3}{8}$

(2) $\frac{5}{8}$

(3) $\frac{7}{8}$

(4) $\frac{1}{6}$

(5) $\frac{1}{10}$

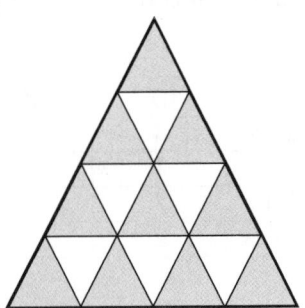

PART II

Directions: Solve the following problems without a calculator.

Problems 16–19 refer to the table below showing the number of men and women in night school held at the Lakeview Community Center.

	men	women
Math	13	17
English	15	21
Spanish	9	17
Word Processing	8	20

16. What is the ratio of men students to women students in the evening classes?

(1) 1:2
(2) 2:5
(3) 2:3
(4) 3:5
(5) 5:8

17. What percent of the students registered for evening classes are taking math?

(1) 20%
(2) 25%
(3) 30%
(4) 35%
(5) 40%

For problems 18 and 19, mark each answer on the corresponding number grid.

18. The evening classes all end at the same time. What is the probability that the first student to leave the building will be a woman from the word-processing class? Write your answer as a fraction.

19. The evening classes also start at the same time. What is the probability that the first student to enter the building in the evening will be a man in the English class? Write your answer as a fraction.

Problems 20–23 refer to the bar graph below representing the maximum speeds of animals.

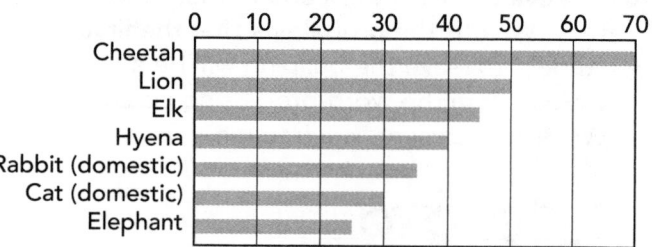

MAXIMUM SPEEDS OF SELECTED ANIMALS

Source: The American Museum of Natural History

20. The maximum speed of the cheetah is how many miles per hour faster than the next fastest animal on the graph?

(1) 15
(2) 20
(3) 25
(4) 30
(5) 35

21. The maximum speed of a lion is about how many times the maximum speed of an elephant?

(1) half
(2) the same
(3) one and one-half times
(4) twice
(5) three times

22. If a hyena ran at its maximum speed for 15 minutes, how many miles could it run?

(1) 5
(2) 10
(3) 12
(4) 15
(5) 20

23. At its maximum speed, a cheetah would need about how many minutes to run 5 miles?

(1) 1–2
(2) 2–3
(3) 3–4
(4) 4–5
(5) 5–10

Problems 24–26 refer to the information below.

A teacher asked ten students each to pick a number from 1 to 10. The table tells the names of the students and the number each student picked.

Sam	10	Kathy	5
Alice	4	Sean	8
June	1	Fumio	7
Mel	7	Shirley	4
Phil	2	Carol	7

24. What was the mean value of the numbers picked by the ten students?

(1) 4
(2) 5
(3) 5.5
(4) 6
(5) 6.5

25. What was the median value of the numbers picked by the ten students?

(1) 4
(2) 5
(3) 6
(4) 7
(5) 8

26. What was the mode (the most frequently chosen) number picked by the students?

(1) 4
(2) 5
(3) 6
(4) 7
(5) 8

Problems 27–31 refer to the graph below showing the number of households in Central County with cable TV from 1975 to 2000.

HOUSEHOLDS WITH CABLE TV

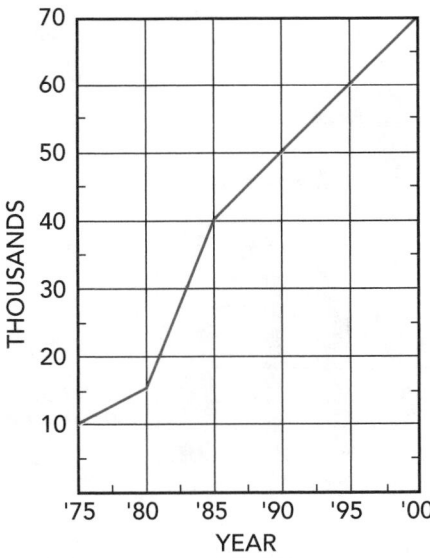

27. About how many households had cable TV in 1980?

(1) 15,000
(2) 20,000
(3) 25,000
(4) 30,000
(5) 35,000

28. In what year did the number of households with cable TV in Central County first reach 50,000?

(1) 1980
(2) 1985
(3) 1990
(4) 1995
(5) 2000

29. To find the percent of increase in the number of households with cable TV from 1985 to 2000, multiply 100% by which of the following expressions?

(1) $\dfrac{40,000}{30,000}$

(2) $\dfrac{70,000}{30,000}$

(3) $\dfrac{40,000}{70,000}$

(4) $\dfrac{30,000}{70,000}$

(5) $\dfrac{30,000}{40,000}$

30. According to the graph, which of the following 5-year periods showed the greatest increase in cable TV hookups?

(1) 1975–1980
(2) 1980–1985
(3) 1985–1990
(4) 1990–1995
(5) 1995–2000

31. If the trend on the graph continues, which of the following best predicts the change in the number of households in Central County with cable TV access for the years 2000–2005?

(1) The number of users will stay the same as in 2000.
(2) The number of users will decrease by about 10,000.
(3) The number of users will double from the number in 2000.
(4) The number of users will increase by about 10,000.
(5) The number of users will triple from the number in 2000.

Problems 32–34 refer to the circle graph below showing the responses to the question, "If you lost your job, how long would you be able to maintain your current standard of living?"

no answer 1%
a week or two 12%
a year 24%
indefinitely 15%
a few months 48%

32. The people who could maintain their living standard for a year was how many times those who could maintain their living standard for a week or two?

(1) half
(2) the same
(3) twice
(4) one and one-half times
(5) three times

33. Those who said a few months were about what fraction of the total?

(1) $\frac{3}{4}$
(2) $\frac{1}{2}$
(3) $\frac{1}{3}$
(4) $\frac{1}{4}$
(5) $\frac{1}{5}$

34. Altogether, 1198 people were interviewed. About how many could maintain their standard of living indefinitely?

(1) 120
(2) 150
(3) 180
(4) 210
(5) 240

Problems 35–38 refer to the following graph.

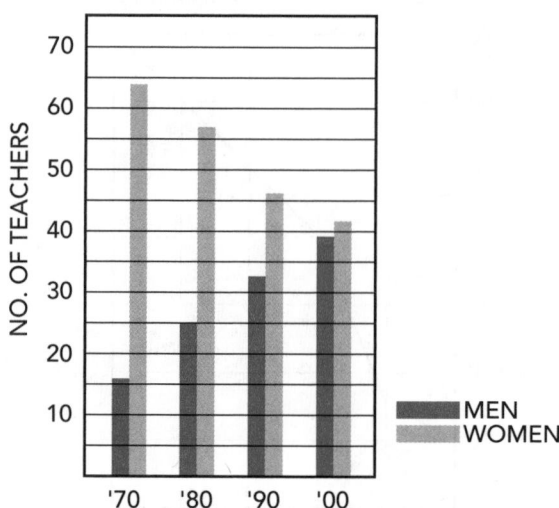

TEACHERS IN GREEN COUNTY SCHOOL SYSTEM

NO. OF TEACHERS

MEN
WOMEN

'70 '80 '90 '00

35. Approximately how many teachers worked in the Green County school system in 1970?

(1) 60
(2) 70
(3) 80
(4) 90
(5) 100

36. Which of the following best describes the change in the number of men teaching in the Green County school system from 1970 to 1980?

(1) The number of men stayed about the same.
(2) The number of men dropped slightly.
(3) The number of men decreased by about 10.
(4) The number of men increased by about 10.
(5) The number of men doubled.

37. Approximately how many women were teaching in the Green County school system in 1990?

(1) 55
(2) 45
(3) 35
(4) 25
(5) 15

38. If the trend shown in the graph continues, which of the following best predicts the number of teachers in the Green County school system in 2010?

(1) The number of teachers will remain about the same, but there will be more women than men.
(2) The number of teachers will increase significantly.
(3) The number of teachers will decrease significantly.
(4) The number of teachers will increase slightly, but the ratio of men to women will remain the same.
(5) The number of teachers will remain about the same, but there will be more men than women.

Problems 39 and 40 refer to the following information.

Ten people agreed to participate in a 6-month study about jogging habits and weight loss. The participants kept a log of the average number of hours they jogged each week. The average hours spent jogging and each person's weight loss are plotted on the scattergram below.

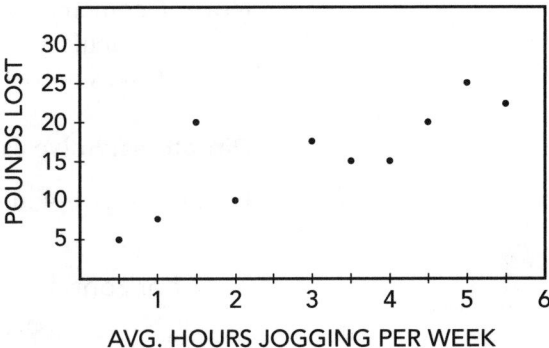

AVG. HOURS JOGGING PER WEEK

39. Each point described below is pictured on the scattergram. Which of the following points conforms *least* to the pattern shown on the graph?

(1) 5 pounds — $\frac{1}{2}$ hour
(2) 10 pounds — 2 hours
(3) 15 pounds — $3\frac{1}{2}$ hours
(4) 20 pounds — $1\frac{1}{2}$ hours
(5) 25 pounds — 5 hours

40. Which of the following best summarizes the data on the scattergram?

(1) There is no relationship between hours spent jogging and weight loss.
(2) More jogging results in greater weight loss.
(3) More jogging results in greater weight gain.
(4) The weight loss for people who jogged 1 to 3 hours per week is about the same as the weight loss for people who jogged 4 to 6 hours per week.
(5) Diet is more important than exercise for weight loss.

Answers are on page 144.

Chapter 9

Basic Geometry

GED Mathematics pp. 223–280
Complete GED pp. 893–921

Basic Skills

Note: Geometry uses many special terms. Be sure you are familiar with the vocabulary in this section before you go on. Use the formulas on page 130 as needed.

Directions: Solve each problem.

For problems 1–4, use the following terms to describe each line or pair of lines.

horizontal   parallel   perpendicular   vertical

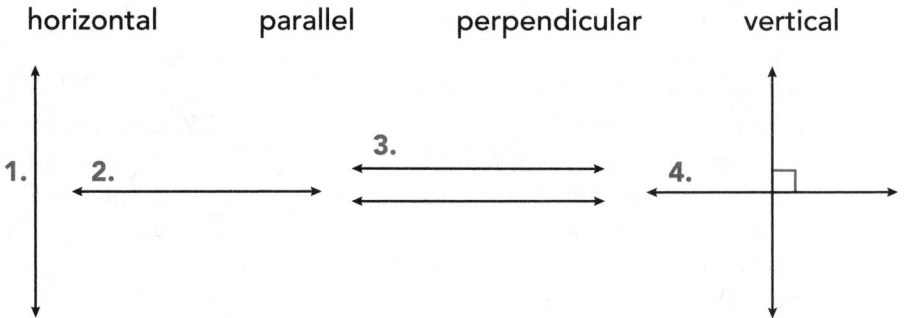

For problems 5–12, use the following terms to describe each angle measurement.

acute   obtuse   reflex   right   straight

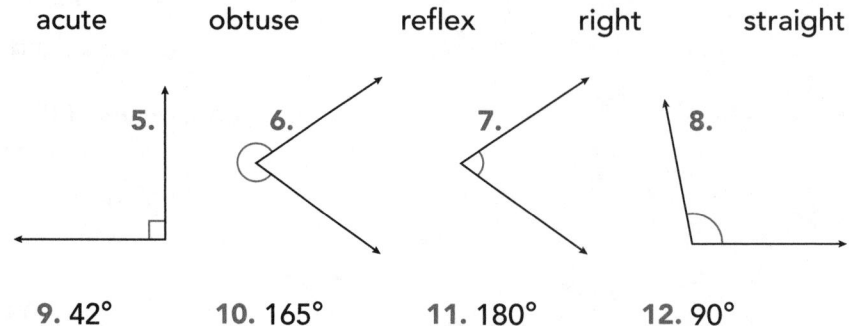

9. 42°   10. 165°   11. 180°   12. 90°

For problems 13–16, use the following terms to describe each pair of angles. Then calculate the measure of $\angle b$ in each figure.

adjacent   complementary   supplementary   vertical

13.

$\angle a = 62°$

14.

$\angle a = 49°$

15.

$\angle a = 75°$

16.

$\angle a = 58°$

For problems 17–24, use the following terms to identify each plane figure.

parallelogram   rectangle   square   trapezoid   triangle

17.

18.

19.

20.

21.

22.

23.

24.

For problems 25–27, use the following terms to fill in the blanks.

area   perimeter   volume

25. A measure of the distance around a plane figure is called the
_____.

26. A measure of the amount of space inside a 3-dimensional figure is called the _____.

27. A measure of the amount of surface on a plane figure is called the _____.

28. Find the perimeter of each figure.

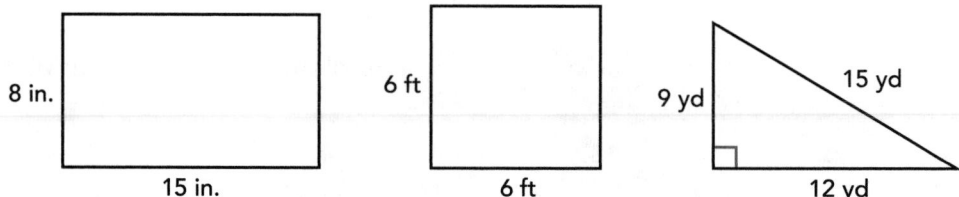

8 in.   15 in.   6 ft   6 ft   9 yd   15 yd   12 yd

29. Find the area of each figure above.

For problems 30–33, use the following terms to fill in the blanks.

circumference   diameter   π (pi)   radius

30. A measure of the distance around a circle is called the
    _____.

31. A measure of the distance across a circle is called the
    _____.

32. A measure of the distance from the center of a circle to its edge is
    called the _____.

33. For any circle, the ratio of the distance around the circle to the
    distance across the circle is known as _____.

34. What is the total number of degrees in a circle?

Problems 35–37 refer to the circle below.

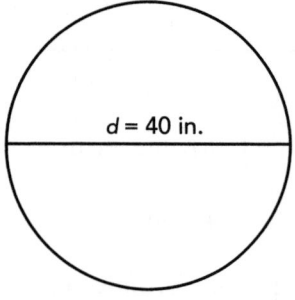

$d = 40$ in.

35. Find the radius of the circle.

36. Calculate the circumference of the circle.

37. Calculate the area of the circle.

For problems 38–43, use the following terms to identify each solid figure.

cone   cube   cylinder   rectangular solid   square pyramid

38.

8 in.   5 in.

4 in.

39.

3 ft   3 ft

3 ft

40.

41.

42.

43.

44. Find the volume of the figure in problem 38.

45. Find the volume of the figure in problem 39.

For problems 46–51, use the following terms to identify each triangle.

equilateral   isosceles   right   scalene

46.

47.

48.

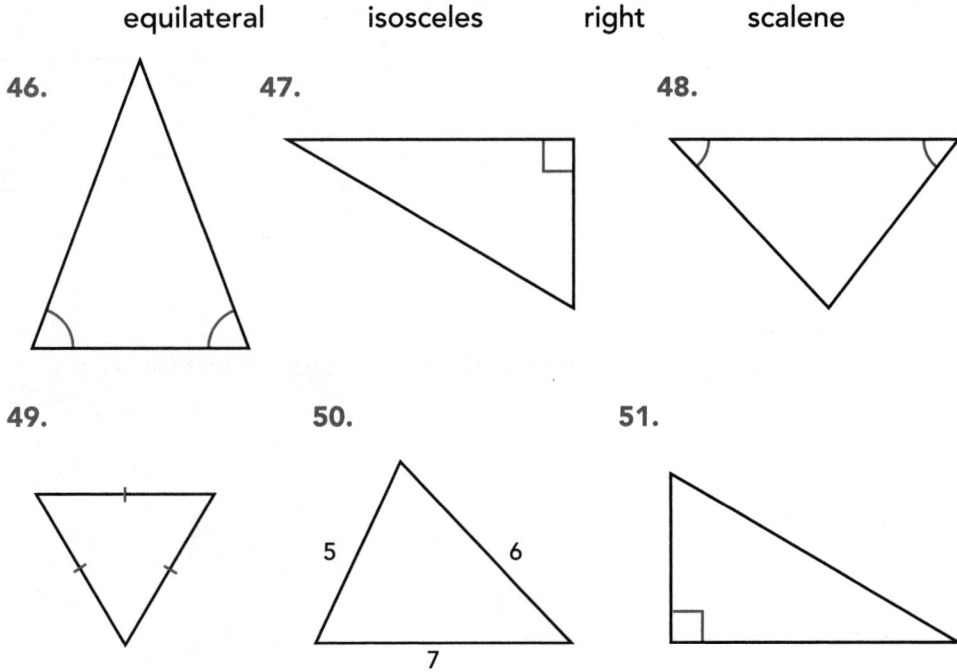

49.

50.

5   6

7

51.

For problems 52–54, use triangle *ABC*, in which $\angle A = 45°$ and $\angle C = 77°$.

52. What is the measurement of $\angle B$?

53. Which side of the triangle is longest?

54. Which side of the triangle is shortest?

55. Are the rectangles below similar? Tell why or why not.

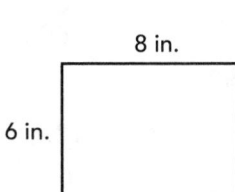 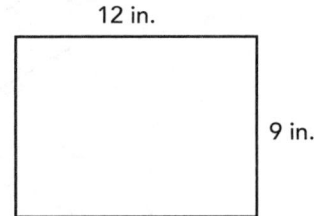

56. Are the triangles below congruent? Tell why or why not.

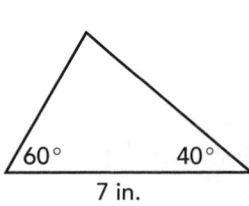 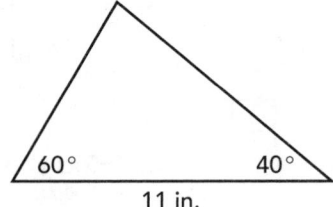

57. Which of the following expresses the Pythagorean relationship for the triangle below?

(1) $5^2 + c^2 = 8^2$
(2) $8^2 - 5^2 = c^2$
(3) $5^2 + 8^2 = c^2$

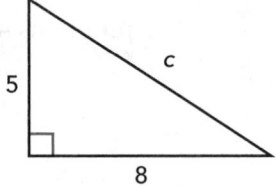

Answers are on page 146.

 Go to **www.GEDMath.com** for additional practice and instruction!

GED PRACTICE

PART I

Directions: You may use a calculator to solve the following problems. Use the formulas on page 130 as needed. For problems 1–3, mark each answer on the corresponding number grid.

1. In the illustration below, ∠XOY = 71.5°. Find the measurement, in degrees, of ∠YOZ.

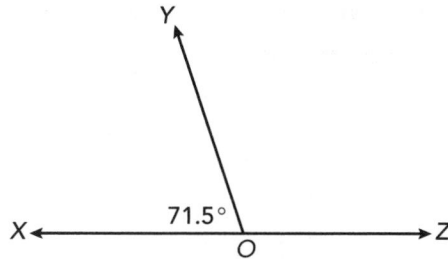

2. A square measures $\frac{5}{8}$ inch on each side. What is the area of the square in square inches?

3. Find the perimeter, in meters, of an equilateral triangle that measures 1.35 meters on each side.

Choose the correct answer to each problem.

4. Find the perimeter, in inches, of a rectangle that is $10\frac{1}{2}$ inches long and 8 inches wide.

   (1) $18\frac{1}{2}$
   (2) 32
   (3) 37
   (4) 42
   (5) 47

5. What is the area, in square inches, of the rectangle in the last problem?

   (1)   80
   (2)   84
   (3)   96
   (4) 144
   (5) 168

6. What is the perimeter, in meters, of the triangle below?

   (1)   9.8
   (2) 12.6
   (3) 15.4
   (4) 16.8
   (5) 19.6

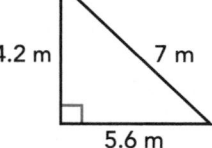

7. Find the area, in square meters, of the triangle in the last problem. Round your answer to the nearest tenth of a meter.

   (1) 11.8
   (2) 12.4
   (3) 15.6
   (4) 19.6
   (5) 23.5

8. To the nearest inch, what is the circumference of a circular tabletop that has a diameter of 30 inches?

   (1) 47
   (2) 83
   (3) 94
   (4) 123
   (5) 188

9. To the nearest square inch, what is the area of the tabletop described in the last problem?

   (1) 283
   (2) 354
   (3) 530
   (4) 707
   (5) 914

10. Find the area, in square feet, of the figure below.

    (1) 162
    (2) 228
    (3) 262
    (4) 324
    (5) 396

    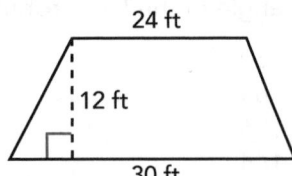

11. Each base angle of an isosceles triangle measures 72°. What is the measurement of the vertex angle?

    (1) 18°
    (2) 36°
    (3) 54°
    (4) 72°
    (5) 98°

12. What is the perimeter, in meters, of a square that measures 0.5 meter on each side?

    (1) 4.0
    (2) 2.5
    (3) 2.0
    (4) 1.5
    (5) 1.0

13. The illustration shows a paving block for a garden walk. What is the volume, in cubic inches, of one paving block?

    (1) 72
    (2) 144
    (3) 216
    (4) 288
    (5) 720

    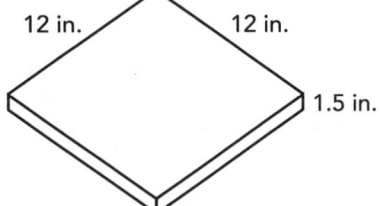

14. One cubic foot measures 12 inches on each side, and one cubic inch measures 1 inch on each side. One cubic inch is what fraction of one cubic foot?

    (1) $\dfrac{1}{144}$
    (2) $\dfrac{1}{360}$
    (3) $\dfrac{1}{1449}$
    (4) $\dfrac{1}{1728}$
    (5) $\dfrac{1}{3600}$

15. To the nearest cubic inch, what is the volume of the cone shown below?

    (1) 262
    (2) 328
    (3) 393
    (4) 524
    (5) 647

    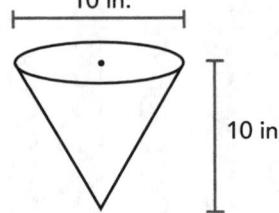

16. Barnstable is directly west of Appleton, and Chatham is directly south of Barnstable. Use the distances in the illustration to calculate the distance, in miles, from Barnstable to Chatham.

    (1) 20
    (2) 24
    (3) 36
    (4) 40
    (5) 50

    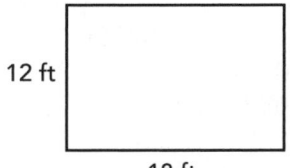

    Barnstable ——— 48 mi ——— Appleton
    52 mi
    Chatham

17. One cubic foot will hold approximately 7.5 gallons of liquid. How many gallons of water are required to fill a pool that is 30 feet long, 20 feet wide, and 5 feet deep?

    (1) 12,500
    (2) 15,000
    (3) 17,500
    (4) 20,000
    (5) 22,500

18. The illustration shows the dimensions of a vegetable garden in the Reeds' backyard. Mr. Reed wants to lay 9-inch-long bricks end to end around the garden. Find the minimum number of bricks that are required to surround the garden.

    (1) 50
    (2) 60
    (3) 70
    (4) 80
    (5) 90

    12 ft

    18 ft

19. The diagram shows the floor plan of the living room and the dining room of the Reeds' home. Rounded to the nearest square yard, what is the combined floor area of the two rooms?

    (1) 32
    (2) 37
    (3) 42
    (4) 47
    (5) 57

    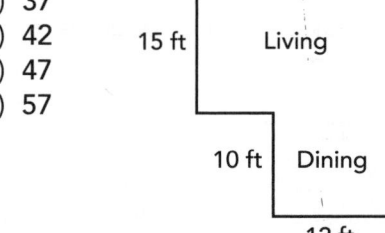

    20 ft
    15 ft   Living
    10 ft   Dining
    12 ft

20. The illustration shows a transplanted tree supported by two sets of wires. The 5-foot-long wire is parallel to the longer wire. Find the length, in feet, of the longer wire.

    (1) 15
    (2) 20
    (3) 25
    (4) 30
    (5) 35

    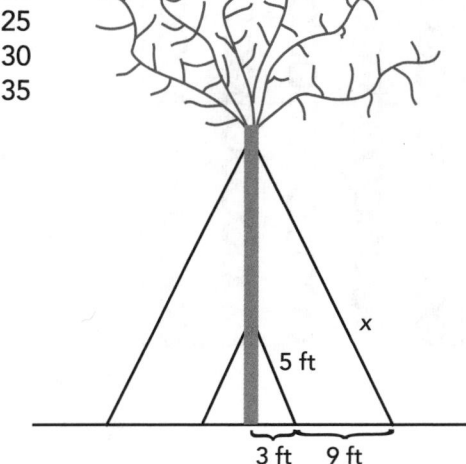

    x
    5 ft
    3 ft   9 ft

PART II

Directions: Solve the following problems without a calculator. Use the formulas on page 130 as needed. For problems 21 and 22, mark each answer on the corresponding number grid.

21. Find the measurement, in degrees, of $\angle x$ in the illustration.

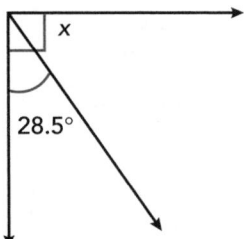

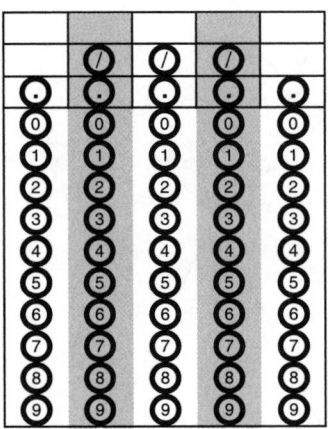

22. What is the area, in square meters, of the figure below?

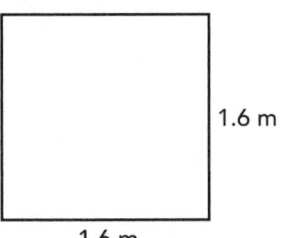

1.6 m

1.6 m

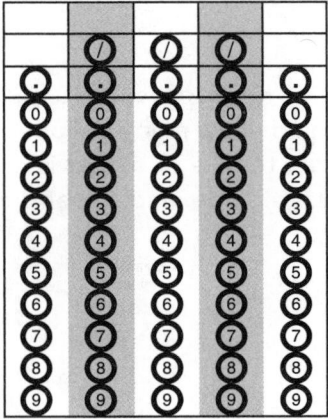

Choose the correct answer to each problem.

23. The illustration shows the dimensions of the side of a barn. Which of the following represents the area, in square feet, of the side of the barn?

(1) $(40)(20) + (40)(35)$
(2) $(40)(20) + (0.5)(40)(35)$
(3) $(40)(35) + (0.5)(40)(20)$
(4) $(40)(20) + (0.5)(40)(15)$
(5) $(40)(35) + (0.5)(40)(15)$

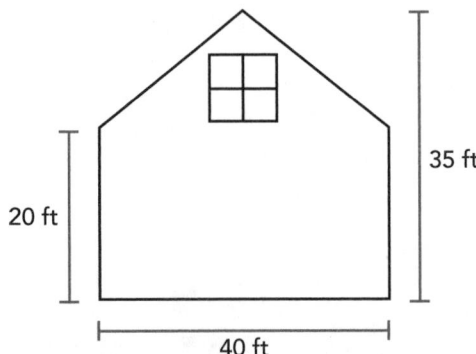

35 ft

20 ft

40 ft

24. In a circle, C represents circumference, r represents radius, and d represents diameter. Which of the following represents π?

(1) $\frac{C}{r}$

(2) $\frac{r}{d}$

(3) $\frac{C}{d}$

(4) $\frac{r}{C}$

(5) $\frac{2r}{C}$

25. In the illustration below $AB = DE$ and $\angle A = \angle D$. Which of the following, together with the given information, is enough to guarantee that the triangles are congruent?

(1) $AC = DF$
(2) $\angle C = \angle F$
(3) $\angle A = \angle E$
(4) $AB = DF$
(5) $\angle C = \angle D$

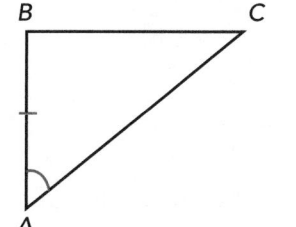 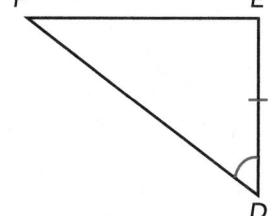

26. Which of the following represents the number of feet of fencing required to go around a circular pond with a radius of 12 feet?

(1) 6π
(2) 12π
(3) 18π
(4) 20π
(5) 24π

27. In the illustration below, line segment CD represents the base of triangle BCD. Which line segment represents the height of triangle BCD?

(1) BC
(2) BD
(3) AD
(4) AC
(5) AB

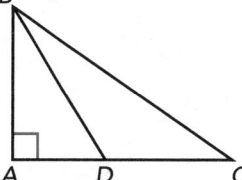

28. In the last problem, $\angle ABD = 42°$. How many degrees are there in $\angle BDC$?

(1) 108°
(2) 116°
(3) 128°
(4) 132°
(5) 158°

29. Tom is building a table for his family's patio. The top of the table will be 6 feet long and 3 feet wide. The surface will be covered with square ceramic tiles, each measuring 4 inches on a side. What is the minimum number of tiles required to cover the top of the table?

(1) 144
(2) 162
(3) 180
(4) 270
(5) 288

30. The vertex angle of an isosceles triangle measures 55°. Which of the following represents the measurement of each base angle?

(1) $90° - 55°$

(2) $180° - 55°$

(3) $2(180° - 55°)$

(4) $\frac{180° - 55°}{2}$

(5) $180° - \frac{55°}{2}$

31. The illustration below shows the concrete slab that will form the floor of a garage. Find the volume of the slab in cubic feet.

(1) 120
(2) 144
(3) 180
(4) 240
(5) 480

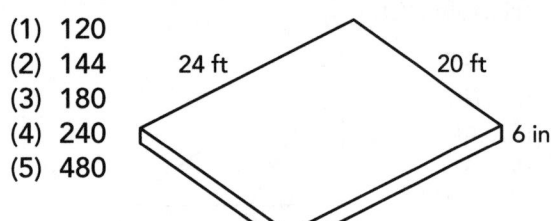

24 ft   20 ft   6 in.

For problems 32 and 33, refer to the illustration below.

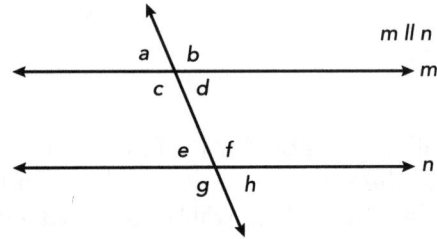

m ∥ n

32. If $\angle a = 57°$, which other angles measure 57°?

(1) $\angle b, \angle c, \angle g$
(2) $\angle d, \angle f, \angle g$
(3) $\angle b, \angle g, \angle h$
(4) $\angle c, \angle e, \angle g$
(5) $\angle d, \angle e, \angle h$

33. What is the sum of angles a, b, c, and d?

(1) 360°
(2) 270°
(3) 180°
(4) 135°
(5)   90°

34. The illustration shows the plan of an L-shaped deck. Which of the following represents the area of the deck in square feet?

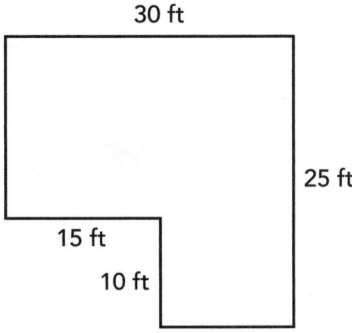

30 ft   25 ft   15 ft   10 ft

(1) (30)(15) + (15)(10)
(2) (30)(25) + (15)(10)
(3) (30)(15) + (25)(10)
(4) (30)(10) + (25)(15)
(5) (30)(15) − (10)(15)

35. The area of triangle *ACE* below is what percent of the area of rectangle *ABDE*?

(1)   25%
(2) $33\frac{1}{3}\%$
(3)   50%
(4)   75%
(5)   100%

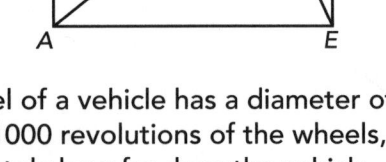

36. Each wheel of a vehicle has a diameter of 2 feet. In 1000 revolutions of the wheels, approximately how far does the vehicle travel?

(1) less than 1 mile
(2) 1–2 miles
(3) 2–3 miles
(4) 3–4 miles
(5) more than 5 miles

37. Fred wants to know the distance across a marsh on his land. The illustration shows a drawing that he made of the marsh and some carefully staked out measurements. $AO = 12$ feet, $BO = 40$ feet, and $CO = 30$ feet. $\angle BAO = \angle DCO$. Use these measurements to calculate the distance DO across the marsh in feet.

(1) 120
(2) 100
(3) 90
(4) 80
(5) 75

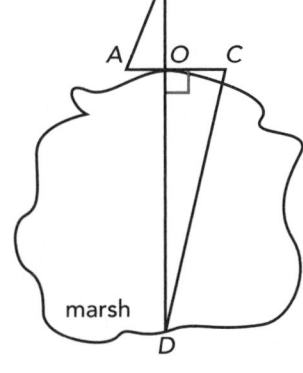
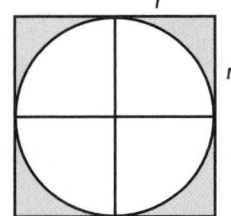

38. The illustration shows a large circle inscribed on four small squares. The small squares measure r on each side. Which expression tells the area of the shaded part of the figure?

(1) $8r - 2\pi r$
(2) $4r - \pi r$
(3) $r^2 - 2\pi r$
(4) $4r^2 - \pi r^2$
(5) $r^2 - \pi r$

39. The illustration shows the dimensions of a building lot and the dimensions of a house that sits on the lot. The house occupies what percent of the area of the lot?

(1) 20%
(2) 15%
(3) $12\frac{1}{2}\%$
(4) 10%
(5) 8%

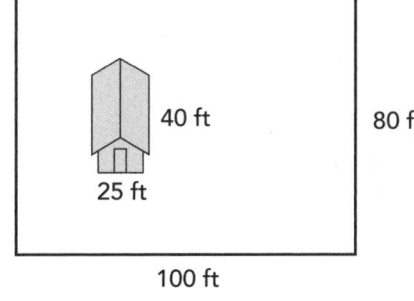

40. Max uses the small cylindrical container (A) to fill the large cylindrical container (B) with water. How many times does Max have to pour the contents of the small container in order to fill the large container?

(1) 8
(2) 16
(3) 24
(4) 48
(5) 64

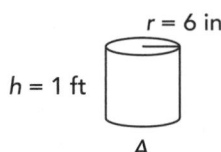
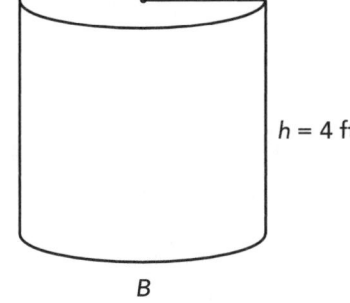

Answers are on page 147.

Chapter 10

The Basics of Algebra

GED Mathematics pp. 281–322
Complete GED pp. 835–872

Basic Skills

Directions: For problems 1–3, fill in each blank with the symbol < meaning "is less than," > meaning "is greater than," or = meaning "is equal to."

1. 8 ____ 0   +4 ____ −6   −7 ____ −3

2. $\frac{3}{3}$ ____ 1   −10 ____ 0 $−\frac{15}{3}$ ____ −5

3. −6 ____ −9 $\frac{18}{2}$ ____ $\frac{36}{4}$ −7 ____ 2

Solve each problem.

4. +8 − 14 =   −2 − 11 =   −3 + 8 =

5. (−7) + (−3) =   −10 + 16 =   (+4) + (−4) =

6. (−3) − (−4) =   (−7) − (+8) =   12 − (−3) =

7. (−4)(+8) =   (−9)(−9) =   (+7)(−10) =

8. $−\frac{1}{3} \cdot 48 =$ $−\frac{2}{3} \cdot −\frac{1}{2} =$ −5 · 0 =

9. $\frac{−20}{−10} =$ $−\frac{18}{24} =$ $−\frac{72}{8} =$

10. 7(4 − 9) =   3(−4) + 7 = $\frac{8 − 20}{3} =$

Solve for the unknown in each equation or inequality.

11. $a + 7 = 20$ $\qquad$ $8b = 32$ $\qquad$ $\frac{c}{3} = 15$

12. $d - 6 = 12$ $\qquad$ $12e = 9$ $\qquad$ $5 = 2f$

13. $4g - 3 = 25$ $\qquad$ $2h + 9 = 10$ $\qquad$ $2 = 5m - 3$

14. $7n - 2n + 4 = 19$ $\qquad$ $6p = p + 10$ $\qquad$ $9a - 4 = 3a + 20$

15. $3(y - 5) = 6$ $\qquad$ $8x - 3 < 13$ $\qquad$ $2s - 7 \geq 9$

Write an algebraic expression for each of the following verbal expressions. Use the letter x to represent each unknown.

16. a number decreased by eleven

17. four times a number

18. five divided into a number

19. eight divided by a number

20. thirty decreased by a number

21. a number increased by nine

22. half of a number

23. ten less than twice a number

Write and solve an equation for each of the following.

24. A number increased by eight is twenty-three. Find the number.

25. Six less than five times a number is twenty-nine. Find the number.

26. Three more than half of a number equals ten. What is the number?

27. Nine less than twice a number equals the same number increased by four. What is the number?

Write an algebraic expression for each of the following.

28. The letter *a* represents Angela's age now. Write an expression for her age in ten years.

29. Chicken costs *c* dollars per pound. Write an expression for the price of $\frac{3}{4}$ pound of chicken.

30. The Mercers take home *t* dollars each month. They spend 25% of their take-home pay on rent. Write an expression for their monthly rent.

31. Five work colleagues shared lottery winnings of *w* dollars. Write an expression for the amount each of them will receive if they share the winnings equally.

32. Sam weighs *p* pounds now. Write an expression for his weight if he loses 20 pounds.

33. A stereo system originally sold for *s* dollars. Write an expression for the price of the stereo if it is on sale for 15% off.

34. A pair of boots costs *b* dollars. Write an expression for the price of the boots, including 6% sales tax.

35. The length of a rectangle is six feet greater than the width. If *w* represents the width, write an expression for the length.

Answers are on page 150.

G E D   P R A C T I C E

PART I

Directions: You may use a calculator to solve the following problems. For problems 1–3, mark each answer on the corresponding number grid.

1. Evaluate the expression $10^3 - 12^2$.

2. Solve for c in $c + 3.8 = 5.2$.

3. Solve for x in $8x - 3 = 2$.

Choose the correct answer to each problem.

4. Simplify $14 - 9 + 3$.

    (1)   2
    (2)   8
    (3) 11
    (4) 18
    (5) 26

5. Simplify $7m - 12 - 2m + 8$.

    (1) $5m + 4$
    (2) $5m - 4$
    (3) $9m - 4$
    (4) $19m + 6$
    (5) $5m - 20$

6. What is the value of the expression $2n - 10$ when $n = -3$?

    (1) -4
    (2) $+6$
    (3) $+4$
    (4) $+16$
    (5) -16

7. Simplify $23 + (-9) - (-5)$.

(1) 9
(2) 11
(3) 19
(4) 32
(5) 37

8. If $a = \frac{1}{2}$, what is the value of $6a - 7$?

(1) $a = 4$
(2) $a = -4$
(3) $a = 4.5$
(4) $a = 6.5$
(5) $a = -6.5$

9. Solve for s in $6s - 1 = 2s + 1$.

(1) $s = 2$
(2) $s = 1$
(3) $s = \frac{2}{3}$
(4) $s = \frac{1}{2}$
(5) $s = \frac{1}{3}$

10. Solve for y in $5(y - 4) = 2(y + 5)$.

(1) 10
(2) 8
(3) 7
(4) 6
(5) 5

11. A triangle has an area of 128 square inches. The base of the triangle measures 16 inches. Find the height of the triangle in inches.

(1) 8
(2) 16
(3) 20
(4) 24
(5) 32

12. For the figures shown below, the area of the square equals the area of the rectangle. Find the length of the rectangle.

(1) 50
(2) 48
(3) 40
(4) 36
(5) 32

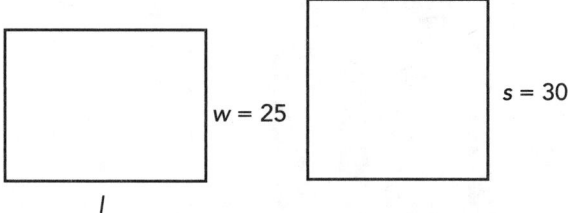

13. A rectangle with side l and width w has the same area as a square with side s. Write a formula for finding the length of the rectangle if you already know the width of the rectangle and the side of the square.

(1) $l = \frac{s^2}{w}$
(2) $l = \frac{s}{w}$
(3) $l = \frac{4s}{w}$
(4) $l = \frac{w}{s^2}$
(5) $l = \frac{w}{4s}$

14. Which of the following is *not* equal to $-\frac{28}{16}$?

(1) $-1\frac{3}{4}$
(2) $-\frac{7}{4}$
(3) -1.75
(4) $-1\frac{9}{16}$
(5) $-\frac{14}{8}$

15. Which of the following represents the perimeter of the rectangle below?

(1) $7x + 2$
(2) $8x + 2$
(3) $10x + 4$
(4) $12x + 4$
(5) $14x + 4$

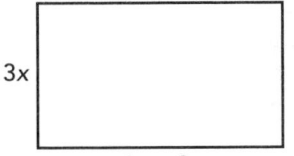

$3x$

$4x + 2$

16. Find the perimeter of the rectangle in the last problem if $x = 5$.

(1) 68
(2) 70
(3) 74
(4) 80
(5) 84

17. Write an equation for "Eight times a number decreased by seven is equal to five times the same number increased by twenty."

(1) $8x - 7 = 5x + 20$
(2) $8x + 7 = 5x - 20$
(3) $8x + 5x = 20 - 7$
(4) $8 - 7x = 5 + 20x$
(5) $7x - 8 = 20x + 5$

18. What is the solution to the equation in the last problem?

(1) 5
(2) 7
(3) 9
(4) 12
(5) 15

19. One season a baseball team won 6 more games than they lost. Altogether, they played 162 games. How many games did they win?

(1) 72
(2) 78
(3) 81
(4) 84
(5) 86

20. Steve makes $42 a week more than his wife, Karen. Karen's father, Joe, who lives with Steve and Karen, works part-time and makes $150 a week less than Karen. Together, the three of them bring home $1212 a week. How much does Steve make each week?

(1) $440
(2) $482
(3) $492
(4) $504
(5) $524

PART II

Directions: Solve the following problems without a calculator. For problems 21 and 22, mark each answer on the corresponding number grid.

21. Simplify $\frac{3^2}{21 - 6}$.

22. Evaluate $(-1.4)^2$.

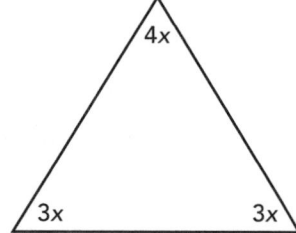

Choose the correct answer to each problem.

23. Which of the following represents the length of the line segment below?

$$\overset{x+2 \qquad x-1 \qquad\qquad 3x}{\vdash\!\!—\!\!+\!\!—\!\!+\!\!—\!\!—\!\!—\!\!\dashv}$$

(1) $5x + 1$
(2) $5x - 1$
(3) $4x + 1$
(4) $4x - 3$
(5) $3x - 3$

24. According to the last problem, what is the length of the line segment if $x = 7$?

(1) 70
(2) 36
(3) 34
(4) 27
(5) 13

25. Find the measure of the vertex angle in the illustration.

(1) 18°
(2) 36°
(3) 45°
(4) 52°
(5) 72°

4x

3x   3x

26. Which of the following is *not* a solution to $5n - 4 \le 11$?

(1) –4
(2) –2
(3) 2
(4) 3
(5) 4

27. Let w represent Ben's hourly wage when he started working at Bash Electronics. Ben now makes $3 an hour more than twice his starting wage. Which expression represents his wage now?

(1) $3w$
(2) $2w$
(3) $2w + 3$
(4) $3w + 2$
(5) $2w + 1$

28. Ben, in the last problem, now makes $18 an hour. How much did he make per hour when he first started working at Bash Electronics?

(1) $4.50
(2) $6.00
(3) $7.50
(4) $8.00
(5) $9.00

29. The table below shows values of x and corresponding values of y. Which of the following equations explains the relationship between x and y for the values shown?

(1) $y = x^2$
(2) $y = 2x$
(3) $y = \frac{x}{2}$
(4) $y = 3x$
(5) $y = \frac{x}{x}$

x	y
1	1
2	4
5	25
6	36

30. Jake drives a truck for a living. On highways he drives at an average speed of 60 miles per hour. Which expression can Jake use to calculate the time t he will need to drive between two places that are a distance d apart?

    (1) $t = 60d$
    (2) $t = \dfrac{60}{d}$
    (3) $t = 2d$
    (4) $t = \dfrac{d}{60}$
    (5) $t = d + 60$

31. By which of the following can you multiply $\dfrac{3}{4}x$ in order to get x?

    (1) 1
    (2) $\dfrac{3}{4}$
    (3) $-\dfrac{3}{4}$
    (4) $\dfrac{4}{3}$
    (5) $-\dfrac{4}{3}$

32. Which of the following expresses the length l of a rectangle in terms of the perimeter P and the width w?

    (1) $l = P - 2w$
    (2) $l = \dfrac{P - w}{2}$
    (3) $l = \dfrac{P}{w}$
    (4) $l = \dfrac{P}{2w}$
    (5) $l = \dfrac{P - 2w}{2}$

33. If m represents Martha's hourly wage now, then the expression $m + 0.1m$ represents her new wage with a 10% raise. Which of the following represents the expression in simplified form?

    (1) $11m$
    (2) $1.1m$
    (3) $0.9m$
    (4) $0.11m$
    (5) $0.01m$

34. Let p represent the regular price of an item in a department store. Which expression represents the price if the item is on sale for 20% off the regular price?

    (1) $0.2p$
    (2) $\dfrac{p}{20}$
    (3) $0.8p$
    (4) $\dfrac{p}{5}$
    (5) $5p$

35. Which equation expresses the relationship between the values in column a and the corresponding values in column b for the table below?

    (1) $b = 2a$
    (2) $b = 2a + 1$
    (3) $b = 2a - 1$
    (4) $b = 3a$
    (5) $b = 3a - 2$

a	b
1	3
2	5
3	7
4	9

36. The formula $c = nr$ expresses the cost of an item, where c represents cost, n equals the number of items, and r represents the price per item. Which equation expresses the cost of an item, including a 6% sales tax?

(1) $c = 0.06nr$

(2) $c = \dfrac{nr}{0.06}$

(3) $c = 1.06nr$

(4) $c = \dfrac{6nr}{100}$

(5) $c = \dfrac{nr}{6}$

37. Which of the following expresses height h in terms of volume V, length l, and width w for a rectangular solid?

(1) $h = Vlw$

(2) $h = \dfrac{lw}{V}$

(3) $h = V - lw$

(4) $h = lw - V$

(5) $h = \dfrac{V}{lw}$

38. Find the measure of $\angle AOB$ in the figure below.

(1) 68°

(2) 61°

(3) 56°

(4) 34°

(5) 18°

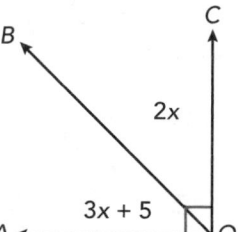

39. A rectangle has a perimeter of 116 feet. The length of the rectangle is 6 feet more than the width. Find the length of the rectangle in feet.

(1) 36

(2) 32

(3) 29

(4) 26

(5) 24

40. A storage container is the shape of a rectangular solid. The length of the container is twice the width, and the height is half the width. Which formula tells the volume V of the container in terms of the width w?

(1) $V = w^2$

(2) $V = 2w^2$

(3) $V = \dfrac{w^2}{2}$

(4) $V = \dfrac{2w^2}{3}$

(5) $V = w^3$

Answers are on page 151.

Chapter 11

Advanced Topics in Algebra and Geometry

GED Mathematics pp. 323–354
Complete GED pp. 835–872, 893–921

Basic Skills

Directions: Solve each problem.

1. Write the coordinates for each point shown on the coordinate plane grid.

   Point A = (,)

   Point B = (,)

   Point C = (,)

   Point D = (,)

   Point E = (,)

   Point F = (,)

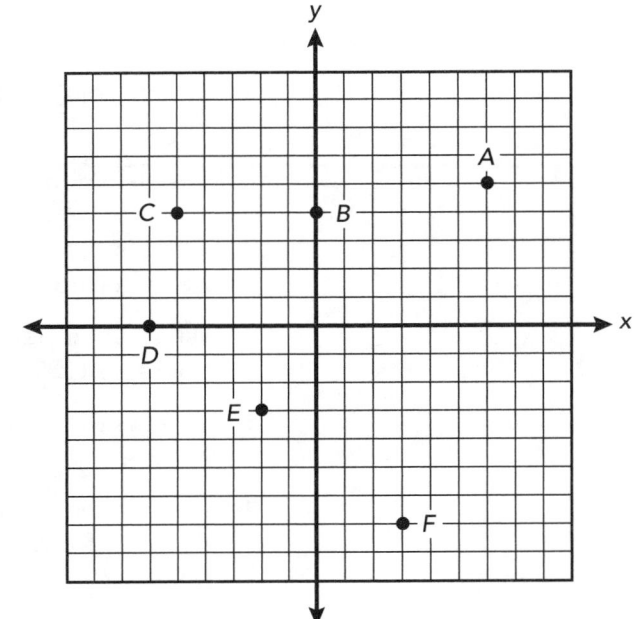

2. Which point in problem 1 lies on the *x*-axis?

3. Which point in problem 1 lies in quadrant I?

4. Which point in problem 1 lies on the *y*-axis?

5. Mark the following points on the coordinate plane grid below.

Point G = (5, 4)

Point H = (−7, 8)

Point I = (−3, 0)

Point J = (−4, −6)

Point K = (0, −6)

Point L = (7, −1)

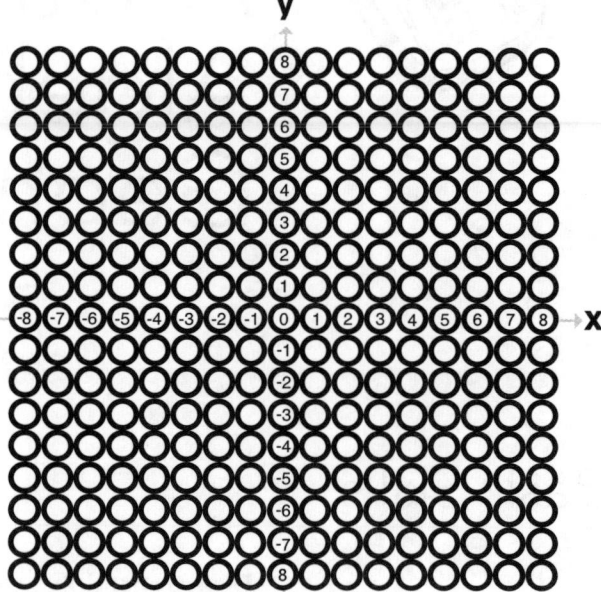

6. Which point in problem 5 lies on the x-axis?

7. Which point in problem 5 lies in quadrant III?

8. Which point in problem 5 lies on the y-axis?

Problems 9–13 refer to the diagram below.

9. What is the distance from point A to point B?

10. What is the perimeter of figure ABCD?

11. What is the area of figure ABCD?

12. What is the diagonal distance from point A to point C?

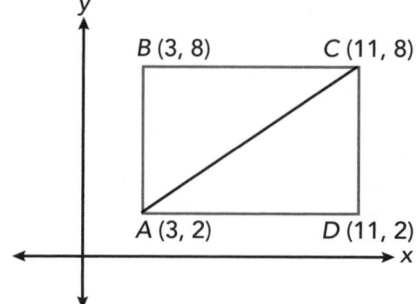

13. What is the ratio of side CD to side AD?

Problems 14–17 refer to the four line graphs below. Match each graph to the descriptions of slope.

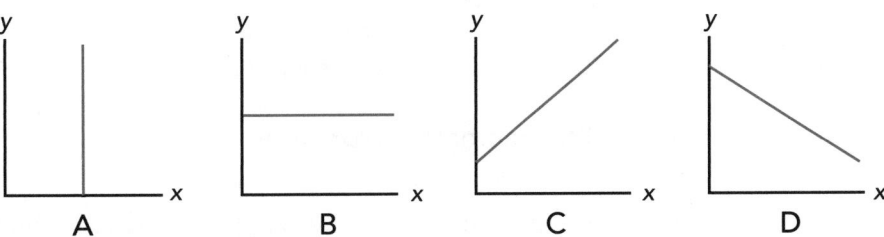

14. positive slope

15. negative slope

16. zero slope

17. undefined slope

Use the equation $y = 2x + 5$ to answer problems 18–21.

18. What is the value of y when $x = 3$?

19. What is the value of y when $x = -4$?

20. What is the value of y when $x = 0$?

21. What are the coordinates of the y-intercept of the equation?

22. What is the slope of the line that passes through points S and T?

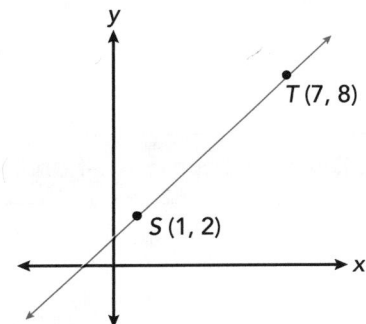

23. Write 48 as a product of prime factors.

24. Simplify $\sqrt{75}$.

25. Simplify $\sqrt{98}$.

26. What is the product of $x \cdot x$?

27. What is the product of $4m^4 \cdot 3m$?

28. What is the quotient of $\frac{c}{c}$?

29. Simplify $\frac{a^5}{a^2}$.

30. Simplify $\frac{12n^3}{6n^2}$.

31. Factor the expression $6x - 4$.

32. Factor the expression $8c + 10cd$.

Use the equation $y = x^2 + 4x + 3$ to answer problems 33–35.

33. What is the value of y when $x = 0$?

34. What is the value of y when $x = 3$?

35. What is the value of y when $x = -5$?

Use the equation $x^2 - 8x + 12 = 0$ to answer problems 36–38.

36. Is $x = 6$ a solution to the equation?

37. Is $x = 3$ a solution to the equation?

38. Is $x = 2$ a solution to the equation?

Answers are on page 153.

 Go to **www.GEDMath.com** for additional practice and instruction!

GED PRACTICE

PART I

Directions: You may use a calculator to solve the following problems. For problems 1–3, mark each answer on the corresponding coordinate plane grid.

1. Mark the point (4, −6) on the coordinate plane grid.

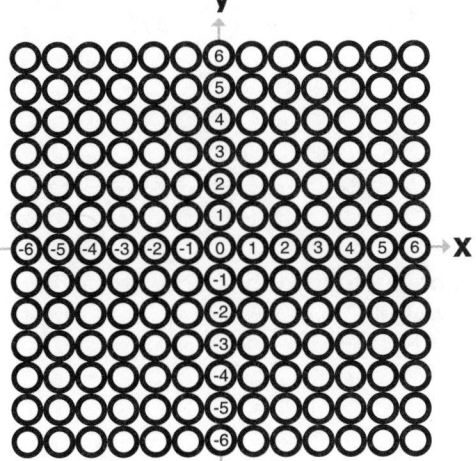

2. Mark the point (−3, −5) on the coordinate plane grid.

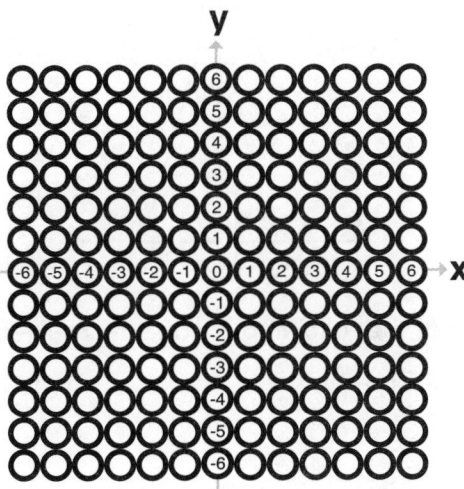

3. Mark the point (−2, 4) on the coordinate plane grid.

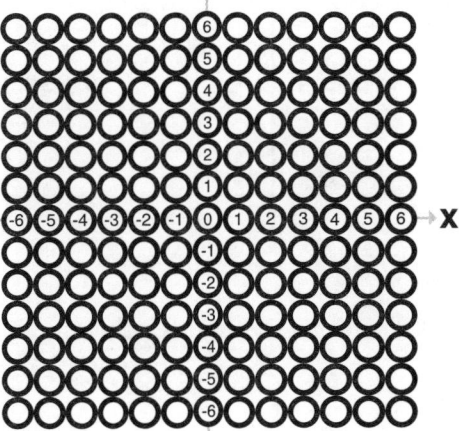

Choose the correct answer to each problem.

4. What are the coordinates of a point that is 20 units to the left of point *C* and lies on a line that is parallel to the *x*-axis?

   (1) (12, −8)
   (2) (12, −5)
   (3) (−5, 12)
   (4) (−8, 15)
   (5) (6, 7)

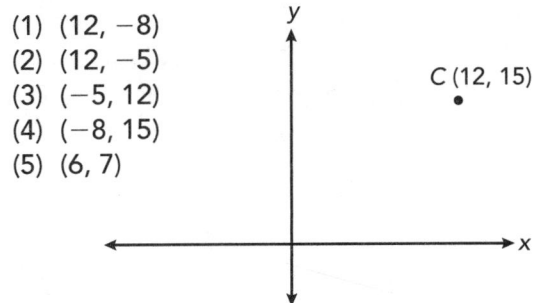

5. In problem 4, what are the coordinates of a point that is 18 units below point *C* and lies on a line that is parallel to the *y*-axis?

   (1) (12, −3)
   (2) (15, −6)
   (3) (−6, 15)
   (4) (−3, 15)
   (5) (−3, 12)

6. What is the distance from point *A* to point *B*?

(1) 10
(2) 12
(3) 13
(4) 14
(5) 15

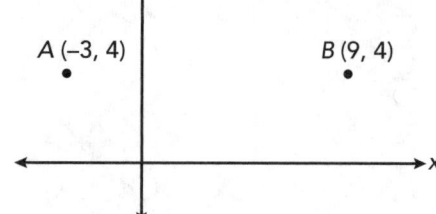

Problems 7–9 refer to the figure below.

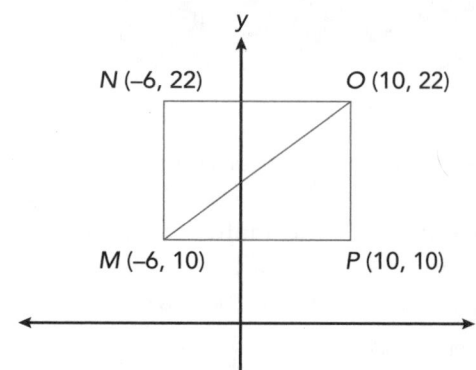

7. What is the perimeter of rectangle *MNOP*?

(1) 20
(2) 28
(3) 40
(4) 48
(5) 56

8. What is the area of rectangle *MNOP*?

(1) 96
(2) 128
(3) 160
(4) 192
(5) 240

9. What is the diagonal distance from point *M* to point *O*?

(1) 12
(2) 16
(3) 20
(4) 24
(5) 28

10. What is the value of *y* for the equation $y = x^2 - x$ when $x = 12$?

(1) 104
(2) 124
(3) 132
(4) 144
(5) 156

11. What is the value of *y* for the equation $y = x^2 - 5x + 2$ when $x = -3$?

(1) −8
(2) −4
(3) 4
(4) 8
(5) 26

12. Which of the following is equal to $3ab \cdot 4a^2b^3$?

(1) $12ab$
(2) $12a^3b^4$
(3) $12a^2b^3$
(4) $7ab$
(5) $7a^2b^3$

13. Find the area of the triangle below.

(1) $3x^2$
(2) $6x$
(3) $6x^2$
(4) $12x$
(5) $12x^2$

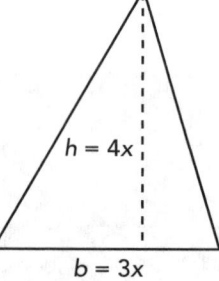

14. Which of the following is equal to $7n(n - 5)$?

(1) $7n^2 - 7n$
(2) $7n - 5$
(3) $7n - 35$
(4) $7n^2 - 5n$
(5) $7n^2 - 35n$

15. Find the slope of the line that passes through points *S* and *T*.

(1) $\frac{2}{3}$

(2) $\frac{3}{4}$

(3) $\frac{4}{5}$

(4) $\frac{5}{9}$

(5) $\frac{6}{7}$

16. Simplify $\sqrt{175}$.

(1) $5\sqrt{7}$
(2) $7\sqrt{5}$
(3) 57
(4) $5\sqrt{9}$
(5) $9\sqrt{5}$

17. According to a mathematical table, the ratio of the opposite side to the adjacent side of a 60° angle in a right triangle is 1.732. Use this information to calculate *x* in the diagram below. Round your answer to the nearest foot.

(1) 41
(2) 66
(3) 73
(4) 84
(5) 173

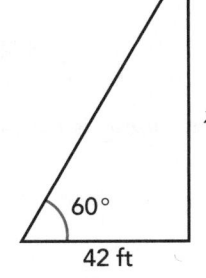

18. What are the solutions to the equation $x^2 + x - 30 = 0$?

(1) $x = 2$ and $x = -15$
(2) $x = 3$ and $x = -10$
(3) $x = 5$ and $x = 6$
(4) $x = 5$ and $x = -6$
(5) $x = -5$ and $x = -6$

PART II

Directions: Solve the following problems without a calculator. For problems 19–21, mark each answer on the corresponding coordinate plane grid.

19. Mark the coordinates of the *y*-intercept of the equation $y = 5x + 4$.

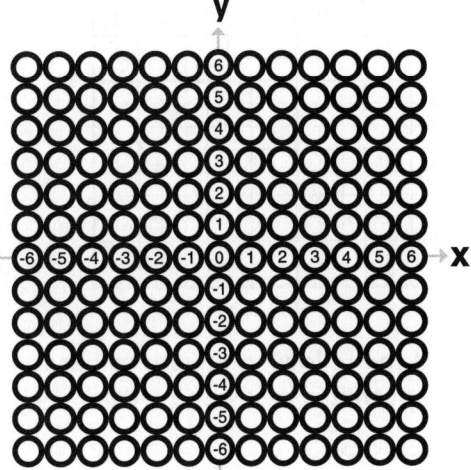

20. The grid shows three points on the coordinate plane. Mark the coordinates of a fourth point that will form a rectangle with a length of 4 and a width of 3.

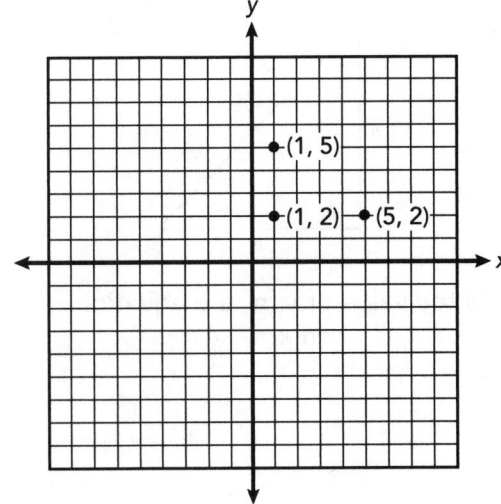

21. The grid shows two points on the coordinate plane. Mark the coordinates of a third point in quadrant III that will form an isosceles triangle with the other two points.

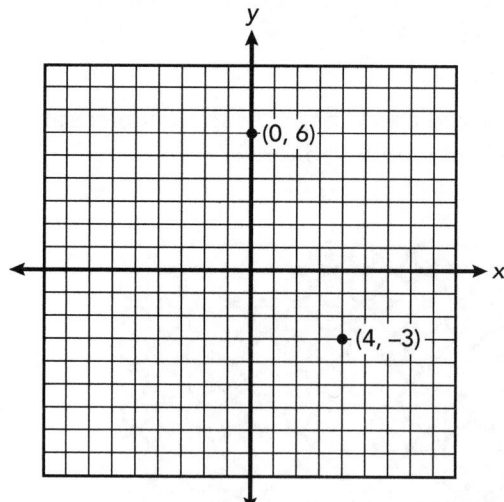

22. Which of the following equations has a y-intercept that is below the x-axis?

(1) $y = 2x + 3$
(2) $y = -5x + 1$
(3) $y = 3x + 4$
(4) $y = x - 2$
(5) $y = -4x + 5$

23. Which of the following represents the length of side AB?

(1) 6
(2) 8
(3) $\sqrt{8}$
(4) $3\sqrt{4}$
(5) $4\sqrt{2}$

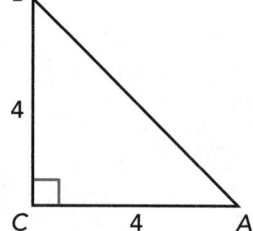

24. What is the value of y for the equation $y = x^2 - x - 6$ when $x = -4$?

(1) −6
(2) 6
(3) 14
(4) 20
(5) 26

25. Which of the following represents 50 as a product of prime factors?

(1) 2×25
(2) 5×10
(3) $\frac{1}{2} \times 100$
(4) $2 \times 5 \times 5$
(5) 4×12.5

26. Which of the following represents the area of the rectangle below?

(1) $12a + 5$
(2) $12a^2 + 5a$
(3) $12a^2 + 15$
(4) $12a^2 + 15a$
(5) $12a + 15a$

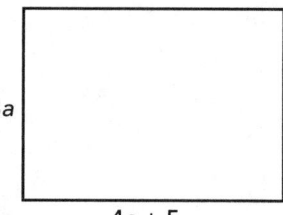

27. What are the coordinates of the y-intercept for the equation $y = \frac{x}{2} - 8$?

(1) (8, 0)
(2) (0, −8)
(3) (−8, 0)
(4) $(\frac{1}{2}, 0)$
(5) $(0, \frac{1}{2})$

28. Which of the following is equal to $9m(2m - 1)$?

(1) $9m - 10$
(2) $18m^2 - 9$
(3) $18m^2 - m$
(4) $9m^2 - 9m$
(5) $18m^2 - 9m$

29. Find the slope of the line that passes through points P and Q.

(1) 1

(2) -1

(3) $\dfrac{1}{2}$

(4) $-\dfrac{1}{2}$

(5) $\dfrac{1}{3}$

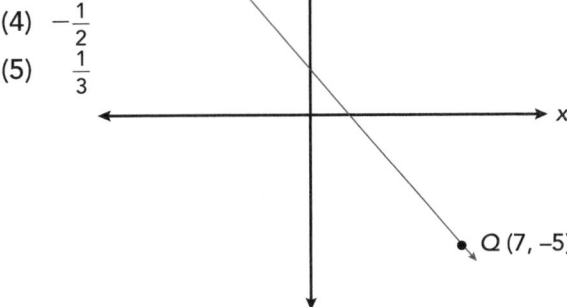

30. Find the quotient of $\dfrac{15m^3n^4}{5mn}$.

(1) $3m^2n^3$

(2) $3m^3n^4$

(3) $3mn$

(4) $10m^2n^3$

(5) $10m^3n^4$

31. Which of the following is a solution to the equation $x^2 - 3x - 28 = 0$?

(1) $x = 5$

(2) $x = 6$

(3) $x = 7$

(4) $x = 8$

(5) $x = 9$

32. What is the distance between point $(4, 5)$ and point $(16, 10)$ on a coordinate plane?

(1) 10

(2) 12

(3) 13

(4) 15

(5) 20

33. Which of the following are solutions to $x^2 + 5x - 24 = 0$?

(1) $x = 3$ and $x = -8$

(2) $x = -3$ and $x = 8$

(3) $x = 4$ and $x = -6$

(4) $x = -4$ and $x = 6$

(5) $x = -2$ and $x = 12$

34. The graph below plots the hours Bill spent studying and the scores he got on four tests. Which of the following ratios *cannot* be used to calculate the slope of the line that would connect the four points on the graph?

(1) $\dfrac{90 - 80}{4 - 3}$

(2) $\dfrac{90 - 70}{4 - 2}$

(3) $\dfrac{80 - 60}{3 - 1}$

(4) $\dfrac{80 - 70}{3 - 1}$

(5) $\dfrac{70 - 60}{2 - 1}$

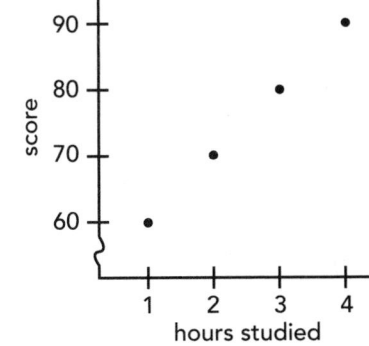

35. What is the slope of the graph in the last problem?

(1) 10

(2) 20

(3) 30

(4) 40

(5) 50

Answers are on page 154.

Mathematics

Directions: This test is similar to the GED Mathematics Test. The test is divided into two sections: Part I which contains 25 questions and allows the use of a calculator, and Part II which contains 25 questions and does not allow calculator use. The formulas on page 130 can be used with both parts of the test. Allow 45 minutes for each section of the Mathematics Test.

At the end of 45 minutes, if you have not completed Part I, mark your place and finish the test. Do the same with Part II. This will give you an idea of whether you can finish the real test in 90 minutes. Mark each answer on the answer grid. Answer as many questions as you can. A blank will be a wrong answer, so make a reasonable guess if you are not sure. Use any formulas on page 130 that you need.

When you finish, check your answers. The evaluation chart at the end of the answers will help you determine which areas to review before you are ready for the actual GED Mathematics Test.

PRACTICE TEST

Practice Test Answer Grid, Part I

1. ① ② ③ ④ ⑤
2. ① ② ③ ④ ⑤
3. ① ② ③ ④ ⑤

4. [grid-in answer bubbles]

5. [grid-in answer bubbles]

6. ① ② ③ ④ ⑤
7. ① ② ③ ④ ⑤
8. ① ② ③ ④ ⑤
9. ① ② ③ ④ ⑤
10. ① ② ③ ④ ⑤
11. ① ② ③ ④ ⑤

12. [grid-in answer bubbles]

13. [grid-in answer bubbles]

14. ① ② ③ ④ ⑤
15. ① ② ③ ④ ⑤
16. ① ② ③ ④ ⑤

17.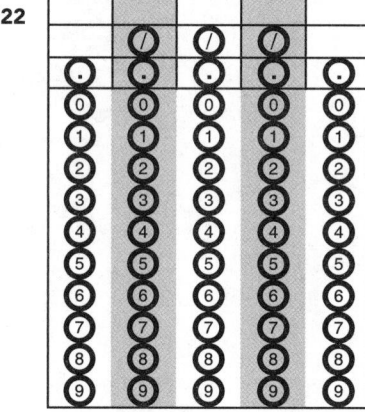

18. ① ② ③ ④ ⑤
19. ① ② ③ ④ ⑤
20. ① ② ③ ④ ⑤

21.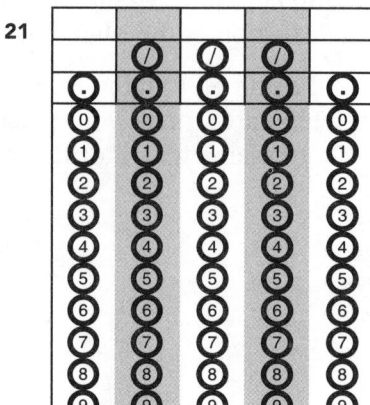

22. [grid-in answer bubbles]

23. ① ② ③ ④ ⑤
24. ① ② ③ ④ ⑤
25. ① ② ③ ④ ⑤

PRACTICE TEST

PART I

Directions: Allow yourself 45 minutes to complete this part of the test. You may use a calculator when necessary. Refer to the formulas on page 130 as needed.

1. In its first year, an Internet company spent $27.9 billion on advertising and made $9.3 billion in profits. What was the ratio of advertising dollars to profits? Reduce your answer to simplest terms.

   (1) 1:3
   (2) 3:1
   (3) 3:9
   (4) 9:3
   (5) 27:9

2. The Consumer Products Safety Commission recently found that 4 out of 5 cribs provided at U.S. hotels are unsafe. What percentage of the cribs are unsafe?

   (1) 75%
   (2) 80%
   (3) 88%
   (4) 90%
   (5) 125%

3. Sue Ellen spent $45.00 on a glass vase for her antiques shop. She wants to make a profit of $4.00 on every $6.00 she spends. Which expression shows the price at which she should sell the vase?

   (1) $45 \times 3\,4$

   (2) $45 \times \frac{6}{4}$

   (3) $\frac{4 \times 45}{6}$

   (4) $45 + (\frac{4}{6} \times 45)$

   (5) $45 + (45 \times 4)$

4. Sue Ellen is buying a new shelving system for her store. She can buy glass shelves that are 6 inches deep and 3 feet wide, or she can buy wooden shelves that are twice as wide and twice as deep. How many times as much space is there on each wooden shelf?

   Mark your answer in the circles in the grid on the answer sheet.

5. Melanie wants to know how far she has driven in one day.

   The drawings below show the mileage gauge on her car at the beginning and at the end of her trip. To the nearest tenth of a mile, how far did Melanie travel?

   Mark your answer in the circles in the grid on the answer sheet.

   Before trip

   | 0 | 1 | 9 | 7 | 2 | 9 | 8. | $\frac{1}{2}\frac{2}{3}$ |

   miles

   After trip

   | 0 | 1 | 9 | 7 | 4 | 1 | 1. | $\frac{5}{6}\frac{7}{8}$ |

   miles

6. Which of the following expressions has the same value as $x^2 \times x^5$?

   (1) x^7
   (2) x^{10}
   (3) $2x^7$
   (4) $2x^{10}$
   (5) x^{11}

PRACTICE TEST

7. In a certain restaurant chain, a serving of macaroni and cheese is $\frac{2}{3}$ cup. Which expression shows how many servings are in a 5-gallon (80-cup) tub of macaroni and cheese?

(1) $80 \times \frac{2}{3}$

(2) $80 \times \frac{3}{2}$

(3) $\frac{80 + 2}{3}$

(4) $\frac{80 - 2}{3}$

(5) $\frac{80 - 3}{2}$

8. What is the slope of the line that passes through points A and B?

(1) $\frac{5}{2}$

(2) $-\frac{5}{2}$

(3) $-\frac{4}{3}$

(4) $\frac{3}{4}$

(5) $-\frac{3}{5}$

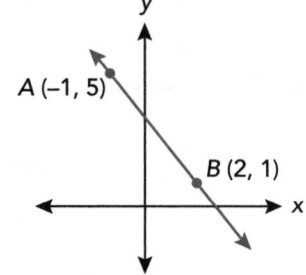

Question 9 refers to the following map.

Kennelworth Park

0.6 miles · Lake · 0.8 miles · 1 mile · 1.8 miles

9. Which is the best estimate of how many square miles of dry land Kennelworth Park contains?

(1) 1.1

(2) 1.5

(3) 1.75

(4) 1.8

(5) 2.1

Directions: Questions 10–12 refer to the following chart.

COST OF RUNNING VARIOUS TYPES OF WATER HEATERS

(To estimate your water heating bill, locate the price you pay for gas, electricity, or propane on the chart below.)

Natural Gas		Propane		Electricity	
Price per therm	Yearly Cost	Price per gallon	Yearly Cost	Price per kilowatt-hour	Yearly Cost
$0.50	$136	$0.95	$283	$0.08	$390
$0.60	$163	$1.05	$313	$0.10	$488
$0.70	$190	$1.15	$343	$0.12	$585

Source: California Energy Commission

10. If the fuel prices shown on this chart are typical, which type of water heater is least expensive to run?

    (1) natural gas
    (2) propane
    (3) electric
    (4) It depends on how much hot water you use.
    (5) Not enough information is given.

11. Which of these graphs best shows the relationship between the price per gallon of propane and the yearly cost of running a propane water heater?

    (1) 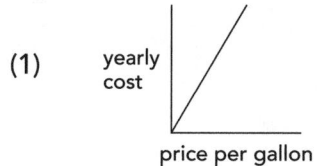

    (2) 

    (3) 

    (4) 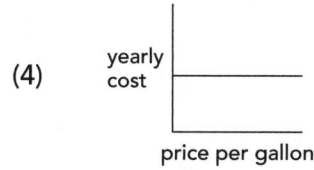

    (5) 

12. What would it cost to run a natural gas water heater for one year in an area where natural gas costs 90¢ per therm?

Mark your answer in the circles in the grid on the answer sheet.

13. Ray is 6 feet tall. One afternoon he measures the length of his own shadow (0.8 feet) and the length of the shadow cast by his house (7 feet). To the nearest tenth of a foot, how tall is the house?

Mark your answer in the circles in the grid on the answer sheet.

14. The owner of Harry's Bicycle Shop is conducting a survey to find out why people shop at his competitor's store. Which of the following would be the best group for him to survey?

    (1) 200 children at local grade schools
    (2) 200 shoppers stopped on a downtown street
    (3) 200 participants in the town's annual bike tour
    (4) 2 people stopped outside the competitor's store
    (5) 1000 people who subscribe to a national magazine on biking

15. The table below shows how people in different age groups responded to the question, "How would you rate the service you've received at Harry's Bicycle Shop?"

Age	Awful	Poor	OK	Good	Great
12 and under	0	5	18	22	35
13-18	20	8	6	34	32
19-25	18	13	19	29	21
26-35	39	31	22	5	3
36 and over	29	23	28	11	9

These data suggest that the staff at Harry's should concentrate most on improving service to people in which age group?

(1) young children
(2) teenagers
(3) young adults
(4) people over 25
(5) senior citizens

16. Suppose you toss three pennies into the air and they land on the floor. What is the probability that two pennies will land heads up and one will land tails up?

(1) 1 chance out of 6
(2) 1 chance out of 8
(3) 2 chances out of 8
(4) 3 chances out of 6
(5) 3 chances out of 8

17. For the equation $y = 3x - 2$, what are the coordinates of a point when $x = 2$.

Mark your answer on the coordinate plane grid on the answer sheet.

Directions: Questions 18–20 refer to the graphs below.

HOUSING BUILT IN 1970

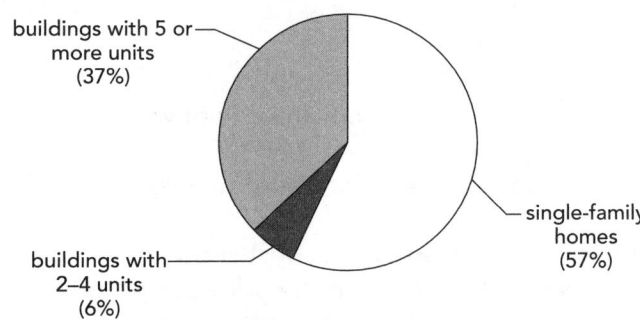

buildings with 5 or more units (37%)

buildings with 2–4 units (6%)

single-family homes (57%)

HOUSING BUILT IN 1998

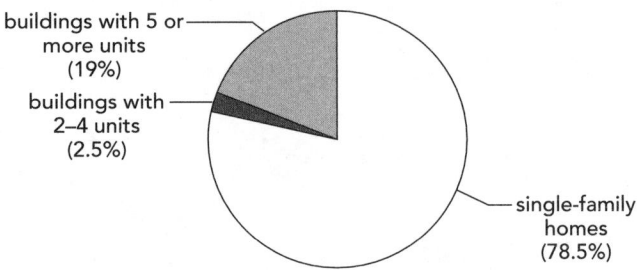

buildings with 5 or more units (19%)

buildings with 2–4 units (2.5%)

single-family homes (78.5%)

18. In 1998, American builders constructed 307,000 apartment buildings that contained five or more units. Which expression shows the total number of apartment buildings and homes constructed that year?

(1) $19 \times 307{,}000$

(2) $307{,}000 \times \frac{19}{100}$

(3) $\frac{19}{307{,}000} \times 100$

(4) $\frac{307{,}000}{0.19}$

(5) Not enough information is given.

19. How many times as many duplexes (2-unit apartment buildings) were constructed in 1970 as in 1998?

(1) 2
(2) 2.4
(3) 3
(4) 3.5
(5) Not enough information is given.

PRACTICE TEST

20. Which of the following generalizations can be made based solely on the data in these graphs?

(1) More housing was built in 1998 than in 1970.
(2) Apartment buildings are less profitable today than in 1970.
(3) People had more money to spend on housing in 1998 than in 1970.
(4) In 1970, there were more people living in houses than in apartments.
(5) For every apartment building constructed in 1998, nearly four houses were built.

21. When Sheetal drives 80 kilometers per hour, it takes her 4 hours to get to her mother's house. To the nearest tenth of an hour, how many hours would it take her if she drove 100 kilometers per hour?

Mark your answer in the circles in the grid on the answer sheet.

Directions: Question 22 refers to the following diagram.

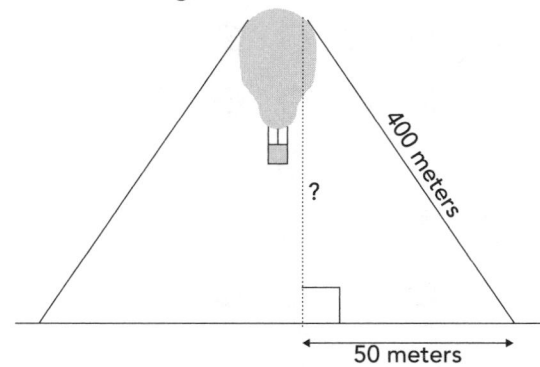

22. This hot-air balloon is anchored to the ground with 400-meter cables. About how many meters above the ground is the top of the balloon? Round your answer to the nearest whole meter.

Mark your answer in the circles in the grid on the answer sheet.

23. Yolanda's new living room is 180 inches long. Which expression shows how many yards that is?

(1) $\dfrac{180}{12 \times 3}$

(2) $\dfrac{180}{12}$

(3) $\dfrac{180}{12 \div 4}$

(4) $180 \times 12 \times 3$

(5) $\dfrac{180 \times 3}{12}$

Directions: Question 24 refers to the following chart.

Monthly Rent	
Studio (no bedroom)	$450
1 bedroom	$575
2 bedrooms	$700
3 bedrooms	$825

24. Which formula expresses the relationship between the number of bedrooms in an apartment (*b*) and the monthly rent charged for it?

(1) rent = $450*b*
(2) rent = $125*b*
(3) rent = $275*b*
(4) rent = $450(*b* + 1)
(5) rent = $450 + $125*b*

25. Ten thousand shares of stock have been issued for Wise Electronics. A businessman owns 1,345 shares now. He wants to own 51% of the company's stock. Which expression shows how many shares he must buy?

(1) $\dfrac{51}{100} \times 10{,}000$

(2) $0.51(10{,}000) - 1345$

(3) $\dfrac{51}{100}(10{,}000 - 1345)$

(4) $0.51(10{,}000) - 0.51(1345)$

(5) $\dfrac{51(10{,}000) - 1345}{100} \times 100$

Practice Test Answer Grid, Part II

26 ① ② ③ ④ ⑤   38 ① ② ③ ④ ⑤

27 ① ② ③ ④ ⑤   39 ① ② ③ ④ ⑤

28 ① ② ③ ④ ⑤   40 ① ② ③ ④ ⑤

29 ① ② ③ ④ ⑤   41 ① ② ③ ④ ⑤

30 ① ② ③ ④ ⑤   42 ① ② ③ ④ ⑤

31 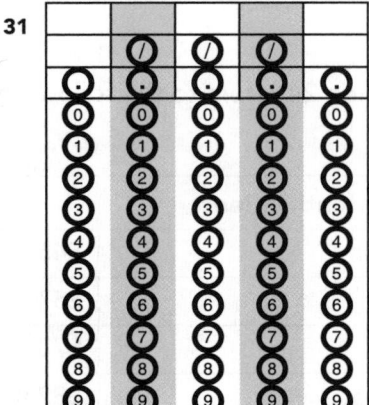   43

32 ① ② ③ ④ ⑤   44 ① ② ③ ④ ⑤

33 ① ② ③ ④ ⑤   45 ① ② ③ ④ ⑤

34 ① ② ③ ④ ⑤   46 ① ② ③ ④ ⑤

35 ① ② ③ ④ ⑤   47 ① ② ③ ④ ⑤

36 ① ② ③ ④ ⑤   48 ① ② ③ ④ ⑤

37 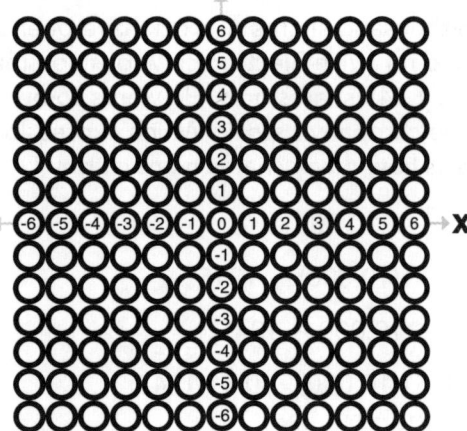   49 ① ② ③ ④ ⑤

50 ① ② ③ ④ ⑤

PRACTICE TEST

PART II

Directions: You are NOT permitted to use a calculator on this part of the test. Allow yourself 45 minutes to complete this part, using paper and pencil to figure your answers. Refer to the formulas on page 130 as needed.

Directions: Questions 26 and 27 refer to the following diagrams which show a triangular cake that must be cut from a cake baked in a square pan.

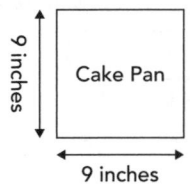 

26. Which option below shows how the final cake must be cut from a cake that is a 9-inch square?

 (1)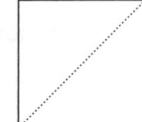

 (2)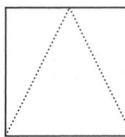

 (3)

 (4)

(5) The cake cannot be cut from a 9-inch square.

27. The baker can be certain that her cake is identical (congruent) to the model if her cake has which of the following?

(1) at least two 9-inch sides
(2) three angles whose sum is 180°
(3) a 45° angle and at least two 9-inch sides
(4) at least two 60° angles and one 9-inch side
(5) three angles identical to the angles in the model

28. Toni thinks that the outer walls of a certain high-rise are perfectly parallel, but a friend insists that they tilt inward. Toni could prove that the walls are parallel if she showed that which of the following is true? (Assume that the walls do not curve.)

(1) The roof is a perfect square.
(2) All four walls are the same height.
(3) There are the same number of rooms on each floor.
(4) The building's shadow is perpendicular to the building.
(5) The walls all form 90-degree angles with the flat ground.

Directions: Question 29 refers to the following diagram.

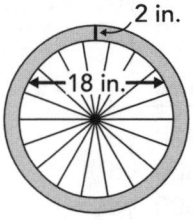

29. To program the computer on an exercise bike, you must enter the circumference of the front wheel. Which expression shows the circumference, in inches, of the bicycle wheel above?

(1) 3.14×6
(2) 3.14×8
(3) 3.14×10
(4) 3.14×12
(5) Not enough information is given.

PRACTICE TEST

Directions: Questions 30 and 31 refer to the following map which shows measurements taken by a naturalist studying the spread of wild garlic mustard.

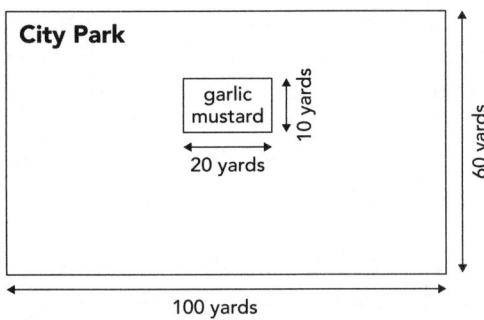

City Park

garlic mustard

10 yards

20 yards

60 yards

100 yards

30. The patch of garlic mustard is doubling in size every 4 years. Which table correctly shows how large the patch will be at various points in the future?

(1)

year	area
4	400 yd²
8	800 yd²
12	1600 yd²
16	3200 yd²

(2)

year	area
1	400 yd²
2	800 yd²
3	1600 yd²
4	3200 yd²

(3)

year	area
4	400 yd²
6	800 yd²
8	1600 yd²
10	3200 yd²

(4)

year	area
4	400 yd²
8	600 yd²
12	800 yd²
16	1000 yd²

(5)

year	area
4	400 yd²
8	800 yd²
16	1600 yd²
32	3200 yd²

31. What fraction of City Park is now covered with garlic mustard? Express your answer in simplest terms.

Mark your answer in the circles in the grid on the answer sheet.

Directions: Questions 32 and 33 refer to the following chart.

Number of Diners at Maxine's Restaurant

	week 1	week 2	week 3	week 4	week 5
Tues.	134	155	102	193	140
Wed.	102	96	131	115	121
Thurs.	167	155	178	182	162
Friday	210	232	264	256	239
Sat.	215	247	256	290	251
Sun.	88	109	100	88	117

32. Which expression shows the mean number of diners on Saturdays?

(1) $\dfrac{290 - 215}{2}$

(2) $\dfrac{290 - 215}{5}$

(3) $215 + 247 + 256 + 290 + 251$

(4) $\dfrac{215 + 247 + 256 + 290 + 251}{5}$

(5) $\dfrac{215 \times 247 \times 256 \times 290 \times 251}{5}$

33. Which of the following is the best prediction of how many diners Maxine's will have next Sunday?

(1) 88
(2) 92
(3) 100
(4) 117
(5) 121

P R A C T I C E   T E S T

34. Between 1997 and 2000, there was a 200% increase in direct payments the government made to farmers. If the government gave farmers $1.8 billion in 1997, which expression shows how many billions of dollars it gave farmers in 2000?

(1) 1.8×3

(2) 1.8×2

(3) 1.8×0.2

(4) $\frac{1.8}{0.2}$

(5) Not enough information is given.

35. A hiker goes to the end of a 2.86-mile trail and back, then hikes an additional 0.23 miles around a lake. Rounded to the nearest tenth of a mile, how many miles altogether did she hike?

(1) 3.1

(2) 4.2

(3) 5.7

(4) 6.0

(5) 6.5

36. Zack just started working out of his home, and he's trying to figure out how much he should charge his clients per hour. On average he should get about 22 hours of work each week, including holidays. Which expression could he use to estimate his yearly earnings at various rates of pay (*r*)?

(1) $r \times 22 \times 52$

(2) $\frac{22}{r} \times 52$

(3) $\frac{22 \times 52}{r}$

(4) $\frac{52r}{22}$

(5) $\frac{22r}{52}$

37. Show the location of the point whose coordinates are (–1, –5).

Mark your answer on the coordinate plane grid on the answer sheet.

Directions: Questions 38–40 refer to the following graph which shows how quickly a potter's kiln heats up.

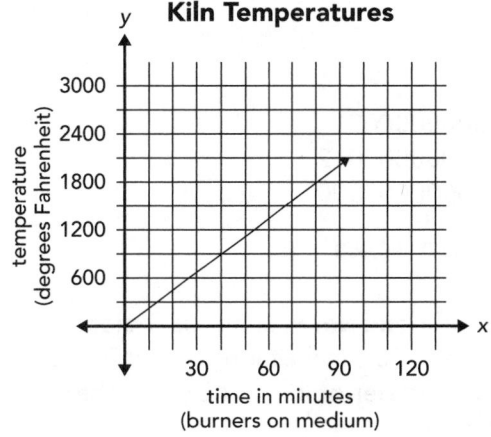

38. If the burners are left on medium for 80 minutes, how hot will the kiln get in degrees Fahrenheit?

(1) 1220°

(2) 1500°

(3) 1800°

(4) about 2000°

(5) Not enough information is given.

39. Which is the best estimate of how hot the kiln will be, in degrees Fahrenheit, after 1 hour with the burners on medium?

(1) 1210°

(2) 1220°

(3) 1250°

(4) 1350°

(5) 1500°

40. If you were to leave the burners on medium for 2 hours, and if the kiln temperature increased at the same rate, how hot would the kiln get in degrees Fahrenheit?

(1) 2400°

(2) 2700°

(3) 3000°

(4) 3300°

(5) Not enough information is given.

PRACTICE TEST

41. In August of 1999, NASA used a slingshot maneuver to shoot a probe into space. That maneuver slowed Earth's rotation by 10^{-12} seconds. Which of the following shows 10^{-12}?

(1) $\frac{10}{12}$

(2) 0.00000000001

(3) 0.000000000012

(4) 0.0000000000001

(5) $\frac{1}{1,000,000,000,000}$

42. To build a bookcase, Paul needs 8 pieces of lumber, each $38\frac{1}{2}$ inches long. What is the minimum number of 10-foot boards that he should buy?

(1) 1
(2) 2
(3) 3
(4) 4
(5) 5

Directions: Question 43 refers to the following diagram.

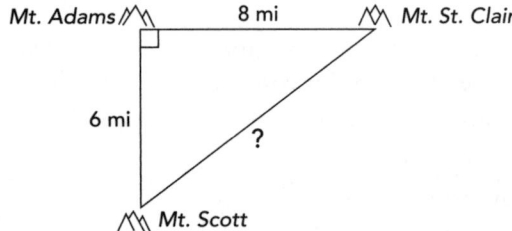

43. Bill wants to hike directly from Mt. Scott to Mt. St. Clair. Use the diagram to determine how far, in miles, Bill will hike.

Mark your answer in the circles in the grid on the answer sheet.

Directions: Questions 44–46 refer to the following graph which shows various settings on a camera. All points on the curve let exactly the same amount of light reach the film. An f-stop indicates the width of the opening into the camera. Shutter speed indicates how long light is allowed through that opening in fractions of a second.

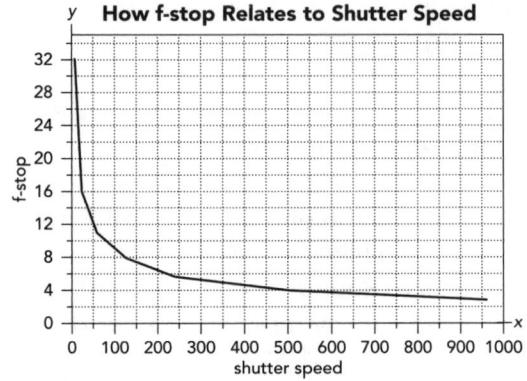

44. On the graph, approximately what f-stop corresponds to a shutter speed of 300?

(1) 4.5
(2) 5.5
(3) 6
(4) 6.5
(5) 7

45. On this graph, every time the f-stop is divided in half, what happens to the shutter speed?

(1) It is multiplied by four.
(2) 500 is added.
(3) It is doubled.
(4) 200 is added.
(5) It is divided in half.

46. What is the x-intercept for this graph?

(1) (0, 1000)
(2) (1000, 0)
(3) (0, 1500)
(4) (1500, 0)
(5) There will not be one.

PRACTICE TEST

Directions: Questions 47–49 refer to the following information.

Nya makes and sells lawn chairs. The materials for each chair cost $18.00, and she sells the chairs for $45.00 each.

47. What percentage of the sale price does Nya keep as profit? (Don't consider expenses other than materials.)

(1) 16
(2) 27
(3) 40
(4) 60
(5) 66

48. Besides materials, Nya spends money on advertising, taxes, and rent. Her total yearly budget for those expenses is $13,400. Which expression shows how many lawn chairs (x) she must sell before she starts making money?

(1) $45x = 13,400$
(2) $x = \frac{13,400}{18}$
(3) $x(45 - 18) = 13,400$
(4) $x = 13,400 \times (45 - 18)$
(5) Not enough information is given.

49. Nya's local lumber yard uses the following formula to determine how much to charge her.

total charge $= pl + 0.12pl - 0.1pl + \$15.00$

l is the amount of lumber Nya purchases, in board feet
p is the price per board foot
0.12 is sales tax
$15.00 is a delivery fee
0.1 is the 10% discount the lumberyard gives local tradespeople

Which expression simplifies this formula?
(1) $16.02pl$
(2) $16.02 + 3pl$
(3) $1.22pl + 15.00$
(4) $0.20pl + 15.00$
(5) $1.02pl + 15.00$

50. Antonio's Pizza would like to start selling square pizzas that require the same quantity of dough and toppings as the round pizzas they sell now. Which equation could the company use to figure out how many inches long to make the sides (s) of each new square pizza? Let d represent the diameter of the old, round pizzas.

(1) $\frac{d}{2} = s$
(2) $2d = s^2$
(3) $\pi d = s^2$
(4) $\pi \left(\frac{d}{2}\right)^2 = \sqrt{s}$
(5) $\pi \left(\frac{d}{2}\right)^2 = s^2$

Answers are on page 126.

PRACTICE TEST
Answer Key

Part I

1. (2) 3:1 $27.9 \div 9.3 = 3$, so the ratio is 3:1

2. (2) 80% $4 \div 5 = 0.8$

$0.8 \times 100\% = 80\%$

3. (4) $45 + (\frac{4}{6} \times 45)$ Set up a ratio to find her profit (x):

$$\frac{4}{6} = \frac{x}{45}$$

Multiply to isolate x: $\frac{4}{6} \times 45 = x$

Final price = cost + profit = $45 + (\frac{4}{6} \times 45)$

4. 4   If the area on top of each glass shelf is xy, the area on top of each wooden shelf is $(2x)2y$, or $4xy$.

5. 113.5 $197411.7 - 197298.2 = 113.5$

6. (1) x^7 $x^2 = x \times x$

$x^5 = x \times x \times x \times x \times x$

$x^2 \times x^5 = x \times x \times x \times x \times x \times x \times x = x^7$

7. (2) $80 \times \frac{3}{2}$ $80 \div \frac{2}{3} = 80 \times \frac{3}{2}$

8. (3) $-\frac{4}{3}$ slope $= \frac{5-1}{-1-2} = \frac{4}{-3} = -\frac{4}{3}$

9. (2) 1.5   The section covered with water is a little less than 0.48 square miles (0.6×0.8). The entire park is 1.8 square miles ($1 \times 1.8 = 1.8$). That means the park must have a little more than 1.32 square miles of dry land ($1.8 - 0.48 = 1.32$).

10. (1) natural gas   The yearly costs given for running a natural gas heater are much lower than the other yearly costs given.

11. (1)

yearly cost / price per gallon

The yearly cost rises $30 for every 10¢ rise in the price of propane. Since this is a steady rise, it should be represented as a straight line with the yearly cost and the price per gallon rising together.

12. $244   The yearly cost of gas heaters rises $27 for every 10¢ rise in the price of natural gas. 90¢ is twenty cents more than the highest value given on the chart, so the yearly cost would be $190 + $27 + $27 = $244.

13. 52.5 $\frac{h}{7} = \frac{6}{0.8}$

$h = \frac{6 \times 7}{0.8} = 52.5$

14. (3) 200 participants in the town's annual bike tour

This group would include a significant number of potential customers.

15. (4) people over 25   For the most part, people in the 26–35 age group and people in the 36+ age group agreed that service was bad at Harry's.

16. (5) 3 chances out of 8

Penny 1	Penny 2	Penny 3	
heads	heads	heads	
heads	heads	tails	←
heads	tails	heads	←
heads	tails	tails	
tails	heads	heads	←
tails	heads	tails	
tails	tails	heads	
tails	tails	tails	

17. (2, 4)   Your mark should be in the upper right-hand section of the grid.

Start at (0, 0). Count 2 units to the right and four units up.

When $x = 2$, $y = 3(2) - 2 = 6 - 2 = 4$.

18. (4) $\frac{307,000}{0.19}$ To find the whole, divide the part by the percent. And remember, 19% is 0.19 or $\frac{19}{100}$.

PRACTICE TEST

19. (5) Not enough information is given.

The graphs don't tell you how many 2-unit buildings were constructed in either year. They lump 2-, 3-, and 4-unit housing together.

20. (5) For every apartment building constructed in 1998, nearly four houses were built.

This graph doesn't tell you anything about the actual number of homes built or about the people living in them.

21. 3.2 Distance = 80 kph × 4 hours = 320 kilometers

New time = 320 k ÷ 100 kph = 3.2 hours

22. 397 $50^2 + h^2 = 400^2$

$$h^2 = 160,000 - 2,500$$

$$\sqrt{157,500} = 396.8627 \text{ or about } 397$$

23. (1) $\frac{180}{12 \times 3}$ Convert inches to feet: $\frac{180}{12}$

Convert feet to yards: $(\frac{180}{12}) \div 3 = \frac{180}{12 \times 3}$

24. (5) rent = $450 + 125b$

The rent is $450 when $b = 0$. After that, the rent increases $125 for every added bedroom.

25. (2) 0.51(10,000) − 1345

Number of shares he needs: 0.51(10,000)

Number of shares he must buy: 0.51(10,000) − 1345

PART II

26. (3) Option (1) would have one side that is too long; (2) would have two extra-long sides, and (4) would be too small all around. But option (3) could work.

27. (4) at least two 60° angles and one 9-inch side

The angles in any triangle add up to 180°, so you can be sure that any triangle with two 60° angles actually has three 60° angles and three equal sides. If one side is 9 inches, all three sides measure 9 inches.

28. (5) The walls all form 90-degree angles with the flat ground.

If the walls all form the same angle with a given plane, they must be parallel.

29. (5) Not enough information is given.

The formula for circumference is π × diameter, and diameter is the width of a circle at its widest point (measured across the circle's center). Neither 18 inches nor 2 inches is the diameter of this circle.

30. (1)

year	area
4	400 yd^2
8	800 yd^2
12	1600 yd^2
16	3200 yd^2

Values in the *year* column increase by 4, while values in the *area* column double.

31. $\frac{1}{30}$ 10 × 20 = 200 sq yd (garlic mustard)

100 × 60 = 6000 sq yd (park)

$$\frac{200}{6000} = \frac{200 \div 200}{6000 \div 200} = \frac{1}{30}$$

32. (4) $\frac{215 + 247 + 256 + 290 + 251}{5}$

To find a mean or average, add up all values in the set, then divide by the number of values.

33. (3) 100 The data for Sundays don't show any trend up or down, so the average (100.4) or median (100) would be the best way to predict future numbers.

34. (1) 1.8 × 3 200% of $1.8 billion is $1.8 billion × 2. If aid increased by 200%, then the figure in 2000 was $1.8 billion + ($1.8 billion × 2), or $1.8 billion × 3.

35. (4) 6.0

$$\begin{aligned} 2.86 & \\ 2.86 & \\ + \; 0.23 & \\ \hline 5.95 & \end{aligned}$$

5.95 rounded to the nearest tenth becomes 6.0

36. (1) $r \times 22 \times 52$ weekly income = $r \times 22$
yearly income = $r \times 22 \times 52$

37. Your mark should be in the lower left-hand section of the grid.

Start at (0, 0). Count one unit to the left and five units down.

38. (3) 1800°   Eighty minutes is represented by the vertical line to the left of 90. That line intersects with the horizontal line labeled 1800.

39. (4) 1350°   After 1 hour (60 minutes), the temperature is halfway between the lines for 1200 and 1500. That's 1350 degrees.

40. (2) 2700°   Use a straight-edge to extend the line out to the point that corresponds to 120 minutes. That point is (120, 2700).

41. (2) 0.00000000001   To find 10^{-12}, start with the number 10 and move the decimal point 12 places to the left.

42. (3) 3   Each board makes $\frac{10 \times 12}{38.5} = 3$ pieces and a remainder. To get 8 pieces, Paul needs 3 boards.

43. 10   Use the Pythagorean theorem $a^2 + b^2 = c^2$.

$8^2 + 6^2 = c^2$

$64 + 36 = 100$

$c = \sqrt{100} = 10$

44. (2) 5.5   The point directly above a shutter speed of 300 is a little lower than 6 on the y-axis. That means that the value is about 5.5.

45. (1) It is multiplied by four.

The regular shape of the curve tells you that there is a pattern. To find it, look at specific examples, like when f-stop drops from 8 to 4 and shutter speed increases fourfold from 125 to 500.

46. (5) There will not be one.

A curve like this will get close to the x-axis, but it will never touch it. After all, the graph shows you how to expose your film to a certain amount of light. If $y = 0$, then no light is allowed in at all.

47. (4) 60 $45 - 18 = 27$

$\frac{27}{45} = 0.6$ or 60%

48. (3) $x(45 - 18) = 13{,}400$
Profits per chair = $45 - 18$
Total profits = $x(45 - 18)$
Before she can make money, profits must equal expenses: $x(45 - 18) = 13{,}400$

49. (5) $1.02pl + 15.00$ $pl + 0.12pl - 0.1pl + 15.00 =$
$(1 + 0.12 - 0.1)pl + 15.00 =$
$1.02pl + 15.00$

50. (5) $\pi\left(\frac{d}{2}\right)^2 = s^2$ The old and new pizzas need to have the same areas, so take the formula for the area of a circle and make it equal to the formula for the area of a square. That's solution (5). Remember, radius always equals $\frac{\text{diameter}}{2}$.

PRACTICE TEST

Evaluation Chart

Circle the number of any problem you answered incorrectly. Then find the starting page of each book to review the skills you need to solve the problem.

Problem	Section	GED Math	Complete GED
	Number Sense and Operations		
9	Estimation	25	742
5, 35	Decimals	75	725
7, 31	Fractions	103	747
1, 13	Ratio and Proportion	137	785
2, 18, 34, 47	Percent	149	793
3, 21, 25, 47	Word Problems	51	702
6	Powers and Roots	32, 34	711
41	Scientific Notation	93, 127	730
	Measurement and Geometry		
23, 42	Units of Measurement	183	873
5	Scales and Gauges	190	889
4, 9, 29, 31	Perimeter, Circumference, Area, and Volume	234	897
13, 26, 27, 28	Triangles, Similarity, and Congruence	263	912
22, 43	Pythagorean Relationship	271	908
	Data, Statistics, and Probability		
10, 12, 15, 18, 19 20, 38, 39, 40, 44	Graphs and Tables	197	820
14, 32, 33	Statistics	217	815
16	Probability	212	810
	Algebra, Functions, and Patterns		
24, 36, 48, 49, 50	Writing Algebraic Equations	294, 306	838
12, 45	Identifying Patterns	197	824
11, 30	Graphing Equations	205, 329	830, 858
17, 37	Coordinate Plane	323	854
8, 46	Slope and Intercepts	331	860

F O R M U L A S

AREA of a:

square	Area = side^2
rectangle	Area = length × width
parallelogram	Area = base × height
triangle	Area = $\frac{1}{2}$ × base × height
trapezoid	Area = $\frac{1}{2}$ × (base$_1$ + base$_2$) × height
circle	Area = π × radius^2; π is approximately equal to 3.14.

PERIMETER of a:

square	Perimeter = 4 × side
rectangle	Perimeter = 2 × length + 2 × width
triangle	Perimeter = side$_1$ + side$_2$ + side$_3$

CIRCUMFERENCE of a circle — Circumference = π × diameter; π is approximately equal to 3.14.

VOLUME of a:

cube	Volume = edge^3
rectangular solid	Volume = length × width × height
square pyramid	Volume = $\frac{1}{3}$ × (base edge)^2 × height
cylinder	Volume = π × radius^2 × height; π is approximately equal to 3.14.
cone	Volume = $\frac{1}{3}$ × π × radius^2 × height; π is approximately equal to 3.14.

COORDINATE GEOMETRY

distance between points = $\sqrt{(x_2 - x_1)^2 + (y_2 - y_1)^2}$; (x_1, y_1) and (x_2, y_2) are two points in a plane.

slope of a line = $\frac{y_2 - y_1}{x_2 - x_1}$; (x_1, y_1) and (x_2, y_2) are two points on the line.

PYTHAGOREAN RELATIONSHIP

$a^2 + b^2 = c^2$; a and b are legs and c the hypotenuse of a right triangle.

TRIGONOMETRIC RATIOS

$\sin = \frac{\text{opposite}}{\text{hypotenuse}}$ $\cos = \frac{\text{adjacent}}{\text{hypotenuse}}$ $\tan = \frac{\text{opposite}}{\text{adjacent}}$

MEASURES OF CENTRAL TENDENCY

mean = $\frac{x_1 + x_2 + \ldots + x_n}{n}$, where the x's are the values for which a mean is desired, and n is the total number of values for x.

median = the middle value of an odd number of _ordered_ scores, and halfway between the two middle values of an even number of _ordered_ scores.

SIMPLE INTEREST — interest = principal × rate × time

DISTANCE — distance = rate × time

TOTAL COST — total cost = (number of units) × (price per unit)

Answer Key

Chapter 1

Whole Numbers, Basic Skills, page 22

1. quotient

2. difference

3. product

4. sum

5. even

6. prime

7. mean

8. power

9. consecutive

10. median

11. 8 20

12. 9 23 31

13. 17 19 23 29

14. 2

15. 6

16. 80 130 3470 5020

17. 300 6400 11,000 4900

18. 129

19. 381,800

20. 317

21. 4880 $90 + 720 + 4070 = 4880$

22. 124,000 $168,000 - 44,000 = 124,000$

23. 42,000 $700 \times 60 = 42,000$

24. 700 $\dfrac{33,540}{48} = 698 + \text{remainder} \to 700$

25. 289 $17^2 = 17 \times 17 = 289$

26. 20

27. 33 $3 \times 17 - 9 \times 2 = 51 - 18 = 33$

28. 12 $\underset{+5}{1} \underset{-2}{6} \underset{+5}{4} \underset{-2}{9} \underset{+5}{7} 12$

29. 67 $\dfrac{71 + 46 + 98 + 53}{4} = \dfrac{268}{4} = 67$

30. 62 $46 \ \underline{53} \ \underline{71} \ 98 \quad \dfrac{53 + 71}{2} = \dfrac{124}{2} = 62$

GED Practice, Part I, page 24

1. 306

$$720\overline{)220,320}$$
$$\underline{2160}$$
$$4320$$
$$\underline{4320}$$

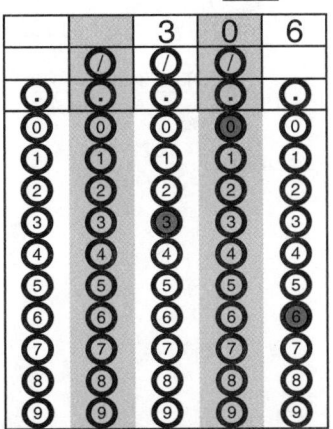

2. 4200 $1300 + 800 + 2100 = 4200$

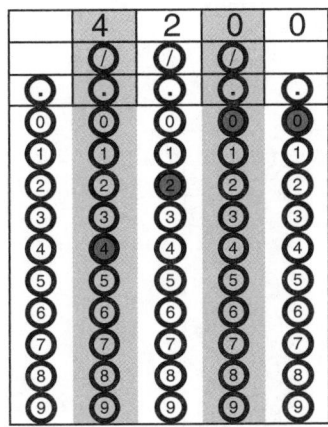

3. 7200 $90 \times 80 = 7200$

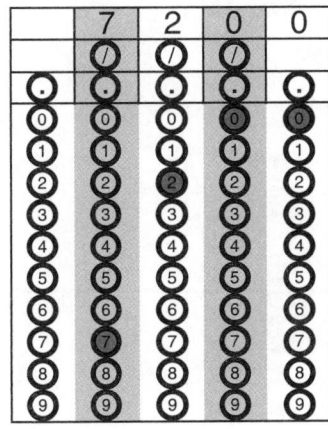

4. (4) $18 \times 18 \times 18$

5. (3) 2304 $48^2 = 48 \times 48 = 2304$

6. (4) 75 $\underset{\times 3}{5} \underset{-5}{15} \underset{\times 3}{10} \underset{-5}{30} \underset{\times 3}{25} 75$

7. (2) 12 $\dfrac{4 \times 30}{26 - 16} = \dfrac{120}{10} = 12$

8. (3) 81 $72 \ 78 \ \underline{81} \ 86 \ 93$

9. (1) $1400 $\underset{-400}{3000} \underset{-400}{2600} \underset{-400}{2200} \underset{-400}{1800} 1400$

10. (2) $207 $\dfrac{\$219 + \$217 + \$185}{3} = \dfrac{\$621}{3} = \$207$

GED Practice, Part II, page 25

11. (4) 20,000 and 25,000   Round each number to the nearest thousand. $3,000 + 2,000 + 16,000 = 21,000$

12. (5) 6400 and 8100 $80^2 = 6400$ and $90^2 = 8100$

13. (4) $6 \times 5 + 6 \times 7$ — This is the distributive property.

14. (3) 70 and 80 — $\sqrt{4900} = 70$ and $\sqrt{6400} = 80$

15. (5) 25 — The other numbers divide evenly into 40.

16. 180 — $\dfrac{10^3 - 10^2}{8 - 3} = \dfrac{1000 - 100}{5} = \dfrac{900}{5} = 180$

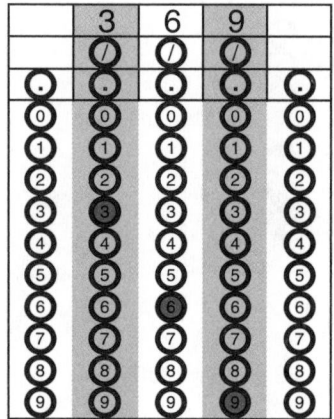

17. 369 — $9(27 + 14) = 9(41) = 369$

18. (1) $r \times r = 5184$

19. (2) 1,820,000 — $1{,}819{,}046 \rightarrow 1{,}820{,}000$

20. (4) Add the scores and divide by four.

Chapter 2

Basic Skills, page 27

1. Operation: subtract
Solution: $14{,}296 - 12{,}783 = 1{,}513$ people

2. Operation: add
Solution: $46{,}597 + 948 = 47{,}545$ people

3. Operation: multiply
Solution: $12 \times \$7.99 = \$95.88$

4. Operation: divide
Solution: $\$5.37 \div 3 = \$1.79$

5. Operation: multiply and subtract
Solution: $8 \times \$1.85 = \$14.80$
$\$20.00 - \$14.80 = \$5.20$

6. Operation: add
Solution: $265 + 418 + 170 = 853$ miles

7. Operation: subtract
Solution: $\$17{,}500 - \$14{,}300 = \$3{,}200$

8. Operation: divide
Solution: $221 \div 13 = 17$ miles per gallon

9. Operation: add and divide
Solution: $65 + 88 + 79 + 92 = 324$
$324 \div 4 = 81$

10. Operation: subtract
Solution: $\$682.40 - \$102.36 = \$580.04$

11. (3) Add their incomes. *Combined* suggests addition.

12. (1) Divide the amount of cloth the tailor has by the amount he needs for one jacket.

13. (2) Multiply her average speed by the time she walks. This is the distance formula $d = rt$.

14. (1) Multiply the price of a ticket by the number of seats.

15. (3) Subtract the weight he lost from his weight last year.

16. Unnecessary information: $20
Solution: $\$10{,}000 \div 8 = \$1{,}250$

17. Unnecessary information: $117 a month for the car
Solution: $12 \times \$814 = \$9768$

18. Unnecessary information: 1000 requests
Solution: $\$14{,}720 \div 640 = \$23$

19. Unnecessary information: 3 crates
Solution: $3000 - 2750 = 250$ pounds

20. Unnecessary information: $1265 in 1999
Solution: $\$1410 - \$790 = \$620$

21. (2) 70×20 — Solution: $72 \times 18 = 1296$ miles

22. (3) $4 \times \$15$ — Solution: $4 \times \$14.79 = \$59.16$

23. (1) $700 - 200$ — Solution: $719 - 189 = 530$ miles

24. (2) $\dfrac{3000 + 3000}{2}$ — Solution: $\dfrac{2683 + 3127}{2} = \dfrac{5810}{2} = 2905$

25. (1) $\dfrac{\$42{,}000}{\$7{,}000}$ — Solution: $\dfrac{\$41{,}670}{\$6{,}945} = 6$

GED Practice, Part I, page 32

1. 392 $28 \times 14 = 392$ miles

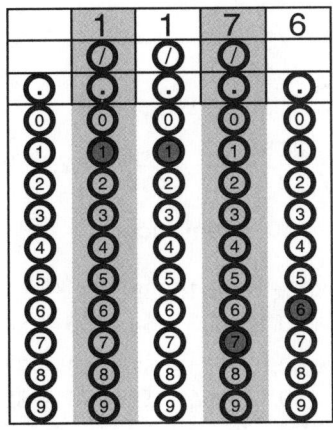

2. 571 $228 + 197 + 146 = 571$ employees

3. 1176 $14,112 \div 12 = 1176$ bundles

4. (3) 102,000 $181,000 - 79,000 = 102,000$

5. (1) $430.74 $6 \times \$71.79 = \$430.74$

6. (2) 907,000 $5,894,000 - 4,987,000 = 907,000$

7. (1) $956.09

$\$1084.27 - \$475 + \$396.40 - \$49.58 = \$956.09$

8. (3) $731,480 $\$1,500,000 - \$768,520 = \$731,480$

9. (4) 40 $\frac{2600}{65} = 40$ minutes

10. (4) $43.26
$3 \times \$3.90 + 4 \times \$7.89 = \$11.70 + \$31.56 = \$43.26$

GED Practice, Part II, page 33

11. 3150 $6000 - 2850 = 3150$

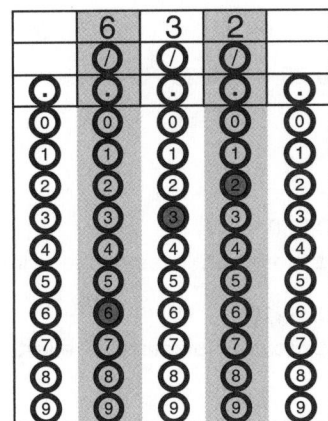

12. 632 $\$200 + 12 \times \$36 = \$200 + \$432 = \$632$

13. (3) about 3 times $\frac{615}{203} \approx 3$

14. (2) $68 \times 4 + 17$
$d = rt = 68 \times 4 + 1 \times 17 = 68 \times 4 + 17$

15. (3) about 750,000   255,772 is close to 250,000.
$250,000 \times 3 = 750,000$

16. (5) 28 $53 - 25 = 28$

17. (5) $718 $2 \times \$359 = \$718$

18. (2) $134
$2 \times \$219 - 2 \times \$152 = \$438 - \$304 = \$134$

19. (2) 2 times $\frac{\$304}{152} = 2$

20. (3) 40 $\frac{500}{13} = 38 +$ remainder $\to 40$

Chapter 3

Basic Skills, page 36

1. 6 7 9   **8.** 0.4 2.4 36.1

2. 5 8 6   **9.** 1.78 0.03 0.20

3. 6 7 9   **10.** 13 6 129

4. hundredths   **11.** 0.08

5. tenths   **12.** 14.007

6. thousandths   **13.** 3

7. 902.735

14. 2.15 + 16.72 + 0.368 = 19.238

15. 2.2 + 16.7 + 0.4 = 19.3

16. 28.726 − 3.42 = 25.306

17. 29 − 3 = 26

18. 32.6 × 5.4 = 176.04

19. 33 × 5 = 165

20. $\frac{0.56}{7} = 0.08$

21. 4.56 ÷ 12 = 0.38

22. 2.844 ÷ 0.36 = 7.9

23. 15 ÷ 9 = 1.66 → .7

24. 25 ÷ 30 = 0.833 → 0.83

25. $(1.4)^2 = 1.4 \times 1.4 = 1.96$

26. $(0.25)^2 = 0.25 \times 0.25 = 0.0625$

27. $\sqrt{0.0036} = 0.06$

28. $\sqrt{0.49} = 0.7$

29. $5.9 \times 10^6 = 5,900,000$
The decimal point moves 6 places to the right.

30. $480,000,000 = 4.8 \times 10^8$
The decimal point moves 8 places to the left.

GED Practice, Part I, page 38

1. 1.77   7.11 − 5.34 = 1.77 million

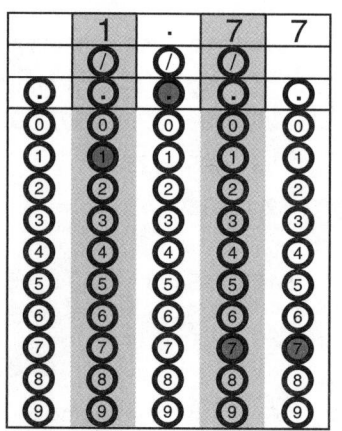

2. 93.1   19.2 + 73.9 = 93.1 pounds

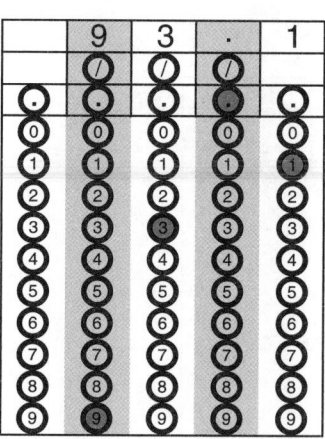

3. 21.9 $\frac{306}{14} = 21.85 \rightarrow 21.9$ miles

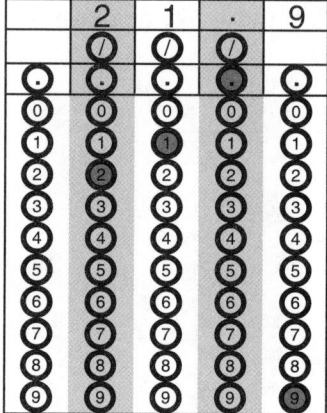

4. (3) 0.269   0.5 × 0.538 = 0.269 kg

5. (4) $5.04   0.87 × $5.79 = $5.0373 → $5.04

6. (2) .338 $\frac{27}{80} = .3375 \rightarrow .338$

7. (4) 39   52 × 0.75 = 39 miles

8. (3) 3.5 $\frac{\$68.60}{\$19.60} = 3.5$ hours

9. (1) 2.15 $\frac{1.2 + 2.55 + 2.7}{3} = \frac{6.45}{3} = 2.15$ kg

10. (1) 30 $\frac{20}{0.65} = 30$ + remainder

11. (4) $43.76   15.0883¢ = $0.150883
290 × $0.150883 = $43.756 → $43.76

12. (2) $1.99   100 × $0.150883 = $15.088 → $15.09
100 × $0.130966 = $13.096 → $13.10
$15.09 − $13.10 = $1.99

GED Practice, Part II, page 40

13. 32.7   964.5 − 931.8 = 32.7 million acres

14. 218.9   2.189 × 100 = 218.9 pounds

15. (1) 30 − 2(12.3)

16. (3) 750,000   1.8 − 1.05 = 0.75 million = 750,000

17. (2) D, E, A, C, B   D = 0.050
                              E = 0.054
                              A = 0.400
                              C = 0.450
                              B = 0.540

18. (3) 1.125   1.875 − 0.75 = 1.125 inches

19. (5) 20 − 2.5(4.99)

20. (3) $38.00   20 × $1.90 = $38.00

21. (5) $5.30   10 × $2.02 = $20.20
                      10 × $1.49 = $14.90
                      $20.20 − $14.90 = $5.30

22. (2) 2.822×10^9 The decimal point moves 9 places to the left.

23. (2) 58,400,000   The decimal point moves 7 places to the right.

24. (3) 584,000 $\dfrac{58{,}400{,}000}{100} = 584{,}000$

Chapter 4

Basic Skills, page 42

1. numerator

2. denominator

3. improper

4. proper

5. mixed number

6. raising to higher terms

7. canceling

8. reducing

9. common denominators

10. inverse or reciprocal

11. $\dfrac{7}{14}$ $\dfrac{11}{22}$ $\dfrac{13}{26}$

12. $\dfrac{7}{9}$ $\dfrac{4}{7}$ $\dfrac{8}{13}$

13. $\dfrac{5}{12}$ $\dfrac{7}{20}$ $\dfrac{7}{24}$

14. $\dfrac{8}{10} = \dfrac{4}{5}$ $\dfrac{6}{36} = \dfrac{1}{6}$ $\dfrac{35}{40} = \dfrac{7}{8}$ $\dfrac{20}{300} = \dfrac{1}{15}$ $\dfrac{18}{100} = \dfrac{9}{50}$

15. $\dfrac{4}{5} = \dfrac{24}{30}$

16. $4\dfrac{2}{3} = \dfrac{14}{3}$

17. $0.035 = \dfrac{35}{1000} = \dfrac{7}{200}$

18. $\dfrac{5}{12} = 0.4166 \rightarrow 0.417$

19. $6 + 6 + 3 = 15$

20. $5\dfrac{1}{2} = 5\dfrac{4}{8}$
        $6\dfrac{3}{8} = 6\dfrac{3}{8}$
        $+2\dfrac{3}{4} = 2\dfrac{6}{8}$
        $\overline{\qquad 13\dfrac{13}{8} = 14\dfrac{5}{8}}$

21. $8 - 3 = 5$

22. $8\dfrac{1}{3} = 8\dfrac{4}{12} = 7\dfrac{4}{12} + \dfrac{12}{12} = 7\dfrac{16}{12}$
        $-2\dfrac{3}{4} = 2\dfrac{9}{12} = \qquad\qquad 2\dfrac{9}{12}$
        $\overline{\qquad\qquad\qquad\qquad\qquad 5\dfrac{7}{12}}$

23. $\dfrac{2}{\underset{1}{3}} \times \dfrac{\overset{15}{45}}{1} = \dfrac{30}{1} = 30$

24. $2 \times 2 = 4$

25. $1\dfrac{2}{3} \times 2\dfrac{1}{4} = \dfrac{5}{\underset{1}{3}} \times \dfrac{\overset{3}{9}}{4} = \dfrac{15}{4} = 3\dfrac{3}{4}$

26. $5\dfrac{1}{3} \div 1\dfrac{1}{3} = \dfrac{16}{3} \div \dfrac{4}{3} = \dfrac{\overset{4}{16}}{\underset{1}{3}} \times \dfrac{\overset{1}{3}}{\underset{1}{4}} = 4$

27. $\left(\dfrac{3}{5}\right)^2 = \dfrac{3}{5} \times \dfrac{3}{5} = \dfrac{9}{25}$

28. $\sqrt{\dfrac{25}{36}} = \dfrac{5}{6}$

29. $0.00038 = 3.8 \times 10^{-4}$
    The decimal point moves 4 places to the right.

30. $2.6 \times 10^{-5} = 0.000026$
    The decimal point moves 5 places to the left.

GED Practice, Part I, page 44

1. $\frac{3}{4}$ $5 - 4\frac{1}{4} = 4\frac{4}{4} - 4\frac{1}{4} = \frac{3}{4}$ ft

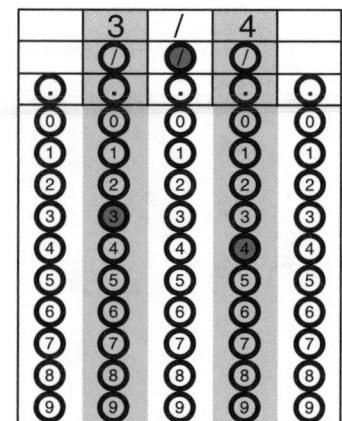

2. $\frac{1}{15}$ $\frac{\$200}{\$3000} = \frac{1}{15}$

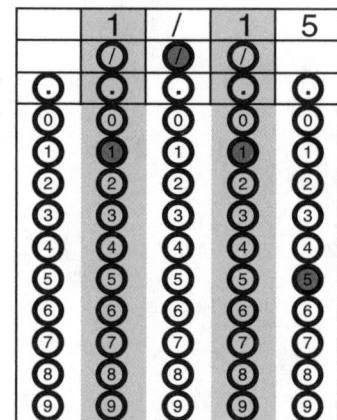

3. $\frac{2}{3}$ $\frac{256}{384} = \frac{2}{3}$

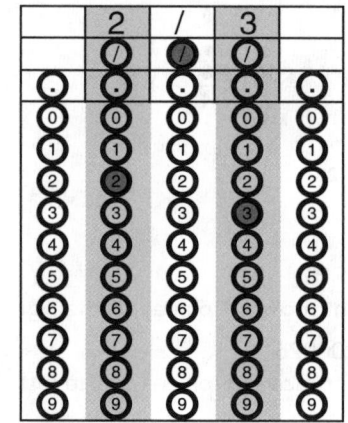

4. (4) 6 $21 \div 3\frac{1}{2} = 21 \div \frac{7}{2} =$

$$\frac{\overset{3}{\cancel{21}}}{1} \times \frac{2}{\cancel{7}} = \frac{6}{1} = 6$$

5. (5) \$9400 $\frac{1}{\cancel{10}} \times \frac{\overset{9400}{\cancel{94,000}}}{1} = \$9400$

6. (3) 16 $12 \div \frac{3}{4} = \frac{\overset{4}{\cancel{12}}}{1} \times \frac{4}{\cancel{3}} = 16$

7. (5) \$5400 $x =$ car loan

$$\frac{2}{3}x = \$3600$$

$$x = \$3600 \div \frac{2}{3}$$

$$x = \overset{1800}{\underset{}{\$3600}} \times \frac{3}{\cancel{2}} = \$5400$$

8. (2) \$1800 $\$5400 - \$3600 = \$1800$

9. (3) $3\frac{1}{3}$ $\frac{5}{1} \times \frac{2}{3} = \frac{10}{3} = 3\frac{1}{3}$

10. (4) \$6 $\$7.50 \div 1\frac{1}{4} = \$7.50 \div \frac{5}{4} = \overset{1.50}{\$7.50} \times \frac{4}{\cancel{5}} = \$6$

11. (4) $\frac{3}{5}$ 48 won + 32 lost = 80 played

$$\frac{48}{80} = \frac{3}{5}$$

12. (1) 62 $4 \times 15\frac{1}{2} = \frac{\overset{2}{\cancel{4}}}{1} \times \frac{31}{\cancel{2}} = 62$ inches

13. (2) 4×10^{-3} $0.004 = 4 \times 10^{-3}$

$$250\overline{)1.000}$$

The decimal point moves 3 places to the right.

GED Practice, Part II, page 46

14. $\frac{7}{8}$ $\frac{21}{24} = \frac{7}{8}$

15. $\frac{11}{12}$ $\frac{1}{4} + \frac{1}{3} + \frac{1}{6} + \frac{1}{6} = \frac{3}{12} + \frac{4}{12} + \frac{2}{12} + \frac{2}{12} = \frac{11}{12}$

16. (4) $800 $2413 → $2400

$\frac{1}{3} \times \$2400 = \$800$

17. (3) $3330 $\frac{2}{3} \times \frac{5000}{1} = \frac{10,000}{3} = \$3333\frac{1}{3} → \$3330$

18. (1) $\frac{3}{8}$ $1\frac{1}{8} + \frac{1}{2} = 1\frac{1}{8} + \frac{4}{8} = 1\frac{5}{8}$

$2 - 1\frac{5}{8} = \frac{3}{8}$ pound

19. (4) $2 \times \$5 = \$10$ $1\frac{7}{8} → 2$ and $\$4.99 → \$5$

$2 \times \$5 = \$10$

20. (4) $4\frac{1}{2}$ $3 \times 1\frac{1}{2} = \frac{3}{1} \times \frac{3}{2} = \frac{9}{2} = 4\frac{1}{2}$ inches

21. (5) 0.000026   The decimal point moves 5 places to the left.

22. (1) $\frac{3}{4}$ $\frac{13}{20} + \frac{1}{10} = \frac{13}{20} + \frac{2}{20} = \frac{15}{20} = \frac{3}{4}$

23. (3) 18 $179 → 180$

$\frac{1}{10} \times 180 = 18$ pounds

24. (2) $26,000 x = price of entire job

$\frac{1}{4}x = \$6500$

$x = \$6500 \times 4 = \$26,000$

Chapter 5

Basic Skills, page 48

1. $16:28 = 4:7$ $6:45 = 2:15$ $72:63 = 8:7$ $8:600 = 1:75$

2. $60 to $100 = $3 to $5   2 to 500 = 1 to 250

75 to 3 = 25 to 1   28 to 56 = 1 to 2

3. $\frac{38}{18} = \frac{19}{9}$ $\frac{1.3}{5.2} = \frac{1}{4}$ $\frac{12,000}{42,000} = \frac{2}{7}$ $\frac{65}{15} = \frac{13}{3}$

4. $\frac{x}{5} = \frac{7}{9}$ $\frac{12}{x} = \frac{5}{2}$ $\frac{1}{8} = \frac{x}{20}$ $\frac{9}{2} = \frac{15}{x}$

$9x = 35$ $5x = 24$ $8x = 20$ $9x = 30$

$x = 3\frac{8}{9}$ $x = 4\frac{4}{5}$ $x = 2\frac{1}{2}$ $x = 3\frac{1}{3}$

5. $\frac{3}{20} = \frac{x}{120}$ $\frac{8}{5} = \frac{100}{x}$ $\frac{x}{45} = \frac{4}{9}$ $\frac{24}{x} = \frac{6}{7}$

$20x = 360$ $8x = 500$ $9x = 180$ $6x = 168$

$x = 18$ $x = 62\frac{1}{2}$ $x = 20$ $x = 28$

6. (5) $\frac{4}{3}$

7. (3) $9 \times 8 = 12 \times 6$

8. (2) $7 \times x = 5 \times 3$

9. new:used $= 21:15 = 7:5$

10. 21 new + 15 used = 36 total

used:total $= 15:36 = 5:12$

11. new:total $= 21:36 = 7:12$

12. 4 right + 1 wrong = 5 total

right:total $= 4:5$

13. $\frac{\text{right}}{\text{total}} = \frac{4}{5} = \frac{x}{60}$

$5x = 240$

$x = 48$

14. 3 grew + 1 failed = 4 total

grew:planted $= 3:4$

15. $\frac{\text{grew}}{\text{planted}} = \frac{3}{4} = \frac{x}{24}$

$4x = 72$

$x = 18$

GED Practice, Part I, page 50

1. $\frac{1}{3}$ $\frac{\text{mortgage}}{\text{other}} = \frac{\$620}{\$1860} = \frac{1}{3}$

2. $\frac{1}{4}$

mortgage + other = $620 + $1860 = $2480 total

$\frac{\text{mortgage}}{\text{total}} = \frac{\$620}{\$2480} = \frac{1}{4}$

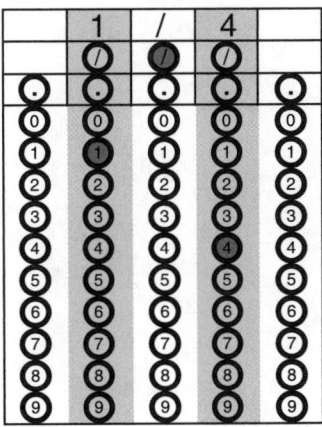

3. $29,760 $2480 × 12 = $29,760

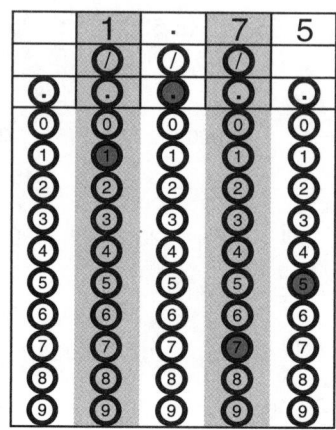

4. (4) $19\frac{1}{5}$ $\frac{5}{8} = \frac{12}{m}$

$5m = 96$

$m = 19\frac{1}{5}$

5. (1) $\frac{2 \times 11}{3}$ $\frac{2}{3} = \frac{c}{11}$

$3c = 2 \times 11$

$c = \frac{2 \times 11}{3}$

6. (3) 24 $\frac{short}{long} = \frac{4}{5} = \frac{x}{30}$

$5x = 120$

$x = 24$

7. (5) $54,000 $\frac{budget}{administration} = \frac{\$10}{\$1.50} = \frac{\$360,000}{x}$

$10x = \$540,000$

$x = \$54,000$

8. (4) 800 $\frac{syrup}{sap} = \frac{100}{2.5} = \frac{x}{20}$

$2.5x = 2000$

$x = 800$

9. (2) 3   yellow + white = 4 + 1 = 5 total

$\frac{white}{total} = \frac{1}{5} = \frac{x}{15}$

$5x = 15$

$x = 3$

10. (5) $3.44 $\frac{oranges}{\$} = \frac{3}{\$1.29} = \frac{8}{x}$

$3x = \$10.32$

$x = \$3.44$

11. (1) 156 $\frac{inches}{miles} = \frac{1}{48} = \frac{3\frac{1}{4}}{x}$

$x = 3\frac{1}{4} \times 48$

$x = 156$

12. (3) $15\frac{3}{4}$ $\frac{inches}{miles} = \frac{1}{20} = \frac{x}{315}$

$20x = 315$

$x = 15\frac{3}{4}$

13. (4) 15:21   The others all equal $\frac{3}{4}$ or 24:32.

14. (5) 21:20 $\frac{7}{8} : \frac{5}{6} = \frac{7}{8} \div \frac{5}{6} = \frac{7}{8} \times \frac{6}{5} = \frac{42}{40} = \frac{21}{20}$

GED Practice, Part II, page 52

15. $\frac{1}{125}$ $\frac{defective}{total} = \frac{80}{10,000} = \frac{1}{125}$

16. 1.75 $\frac{n}{10} = \frac{7}{40}$

$40n = 70$

$n = 1.75$

17. (4) 3:5   9 + 6 + 3 = 18 days of precipitation

18:30 = 3:5

18. (2) $80 $1 saved + $8 spent = $9 total

$\frac{saved}{total} = \frac{1}{9} = \frac{x}{720}$

$9x = 720$

$x = 80$

19. (3) 72 $\dfrac{\text{height}}{\text{shadow}} = \dfrac{9}{2.5} = \dfrac{x}{20}$

$2.5x = 180$

$x = 72$

20. (3) 95 $312 + 193 = 505$

$600 - 505 = 95$

21. (4) 3:2 $312 \rightarrow 300$ and $193 \rightarrow 200$

for:against $= 300:200 = 3:2$

22. (5) 1:6 $95 \rightarrow 100$

undecided:total $= 100:600 = 1:6$

23. (1) 1:2 sand:gravel $= 2:4 = 1:2$

24. (1) 1:6 sand $+$ gravel $= 2 + 4 = 6$

cement:mixture $= 1:6$

25. (3) 290

cement $+$ sand $+$ gravel $= 1 + 2 + 4 = 7$ total

$\dfrac{\text{sand}}{\text{total}} = \dfrac{2}{7} = \dfrac{x}{1000}$

$7x = 2000$

$x = 285.7 \rightarrow 290$

26. (4) $x = \dfrac{4 \times 70}{5}$ $4:5 = x:70$

$5x = 4 \times 70$

$x = \dfrac{4 \times 70}{5}$

27. (4) $4.50 $29.89 \rightarrow 30

$\dfrac{\text{tip}}{\text{total}} = \dfrac{0.15}{1} = \dfrac{x}{30}$

$x = 4.50

28. (3) 96 3 won $+$ 2 lost $= 5$ played

$\dfrac{\text{won}}{\text{played}} = \dfrac{3}{5} = \dfrac{x}{160}$

$5x = 480$

$x = 96$

29. (2) 25 $\dfrac{\text{acres}}{\text{bushels}} = \dfrac{1}{120} = \dfrac{x}{3000}$

$120x = 3000$

$x = 25$

Chapter 6

Basic Skills, page 55

1. $\dfrac{1}{4}$ $\dfrac{1}{2}$ $\dfrac{3}{4}$

2. $\dfrac{1}{5}$ $\dfrac{2}{5}$ $\dfrac{3}{5}$ $\dfrac{4}{5}$

3. $\dfrac{1}{3}$ $\dfrac{2}{3}$

4. $\dfrac{1}{8}$ $\dfrac{3}{8}$ $\dfrac{5}{8}$ $\dfrac{7}{8}$

5. 0.01 0.1 1.0 10.0

6. 0.25 0.5 0.75

7. 0.2 0.4 0.6 0.8

8. 0.08 0.045 0.85 1.1

9. $\dfrac{1}{5}$

10. 2

11. 8

12. 25%

13. 32

14. 35

15. 1%

16. 3500

17. part; $\dfrac{1}{2} \times 66 = 33$ part; $\dfrac{1}{3} \times 120 = 40$

part; $\dfrac{4}{5} \times 35 = 28$

18. part; $0.1 \times 325 = 32.5$ part; $0.4 \times 90 = 36$

part; $0.065 \times 200 = 13$

19. percent; $\dfrac{8}{32} = \dfrac{1}{4} = 25\%$

percent; $\dfrac{19}{38} = \dfrac{1}{2} = 50\%$

20. percent; $\dfrac{10}{200} = \dfrac{1}{20} = 5\%$

percent; $\dfrac{12}{36} = \dfrac{1}{3} = 33\dfrac{1}{3}\%$

21. whole; $16 \div 0.8 = 20$ whole; $17 \div 0.5 = 34$

22. whole; $40 \div \dfrac{1}{3} = 120$ whole; $150 \div 0.6 = 250$

23. 6% $477 - $450 = 27

$\dfrac{\text{increase}}{\text{original}} = \dfrac{$27}{$450} = \dfrac{3}{50} = 6\%$

24. 25% $1200 - 900 = 300$

$\dfrac{\text{decrease}}{\text{original}} = \dfrac{300}{1200} = \dfrac{1}{4} = 25\%$

25. $70 4 months $= \dfrac{4}{12} = \dfrac{1}{3}$ year

$i = prt = $1500 \times 0.14 \times \dfrac{1}{3} = 70

GED Practice, Part I, page 57

1. $\dfrac{3}{20}$ $15\% = \dfrac{15}{100} = \dfrac{3}{20}$

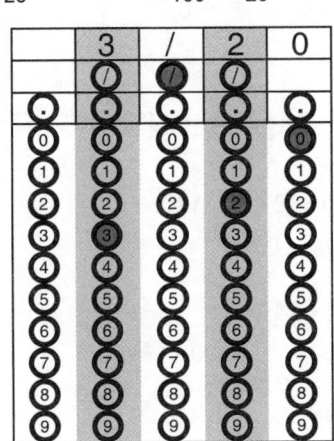

2. 3.48   8.7% = 0.087
0.087 × 40 = 3.48

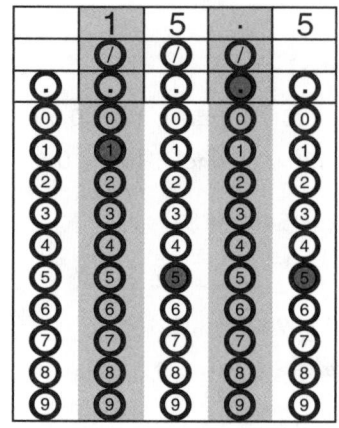

3. 15.5   60% = 0.6
9.3 ÷ 0.6 = 15.5

4. (4) 20% $1.92 − $1.60 = $0.32
$\frac{\text{change}}{\text{original}} = \frac{\$0.32}{\$1.60} = 0.2 = 20\%$

5. (5) 75%   70 − 40 = 30
$\frac{\text{change}}{\text{original}} = \frac{30}{40} = 0.75 = 75\%$

6. (3) $2.25 $7\frac{1}{2}\% = 0.075$
0.075 × $29.95 = $2.24625 → $2.25

7. (2) 1400   15% = 0.15
210 ÷ 0.15 = 1400

8. (1) 6   80% = 0.8
0.8 × 30 = 24
30 − 24 = 6

9. (5) 20% $4500 − $3600 = $900
$\frac{\text{change}}{\text{original}} = \frac{\$900}{\$4500} = \frac{1}{5} = 20\%$

10. (3) $37\frac{1}{2}\%$ $\frac{\text{change}}{\text{original}} = \frac{600}{1600} = \frac{3}{8} = 37\frac{1}{2}\%$

11. (1) $120   4.5% = 0.045
$5.40 ÷ 0.045 = $120

12. (4) $106.25 $8\frac{1}{2}\% = 0.085$
6 months = $\frac{6}{12}$ = 0.5 year
i = prt
i = $2500 × 0.085 × 0.5 = $106.25

13. (4) $1057.88   6% = 0.06
0.06 × $998 = $59.88
$998 + $59.88 = $1057.88
or 1.06 × $998 = $1057.88

14. (2) $898.20   10% = 0.1
0.1 × $998 = $99.80
$998 − $99.80 = $898.20
or 0.9 × $998 = $898.20

15. (3) 153.90   First, 10% = 0.1
0.1 × $180 = $18
$180 − $18 = $162
or 0.9 × $180 = $162

Second, 5% = 0.05
0.05 × $162 = $8.10
$162 − $8.10 = $153.90
or 0.95 × $162 = $153.90

GED Practice, Part II, page 59

16. 1.75   175% = 1.75

17. 2.8   2% = 0.02
0.02 × 140 = 2.8

18. (3) 176

20% = 0.2
0.2 × 220 = 44
220 − 44 = 176

19. (4) 1.06 × $139

The price is 100%.
The tax is 6%.
100% + 6% = 106% = 1.06
The price is 1.06 × $139.

20. (5) $\frac{48}{100}$ The other answers all equal $\frac{480}{800}$ or $\frac{3}{5}$.

21. (1) $\frac{\$2700 \times 0.18}{12}$ 18% = 0.18
$2700 × 0.18 for 1 year
Divide by 12 for one month.

22. (3) 0.9 × $16.95

Original price is 100%.
Sale price is 100% − 10% =
90% = 0.9
The price is 0.9 × $16.95.

23. (3) 50 times faster   To change 5000% to a whole
number, move the decimal
point 2 places to the left.

24. (2) $\frac{115 - 60}{60}$ The change is 115 − 60.
The original membership is 60.

25. (5) 37,500

150% = 1.5
1.5 × 15,000 = 22,500
15,000 + 22,500 = 37,500

26. (4) $32

60% = 0.6
0.6 × $80 = $48
$80 − $48 = $32

27. (1) 700%

$200,000 − $25,000 = $175,000
$\frac{\text{change}}{\text{original}} = \frac{\$175,000}{\$25,000} = \frac{7}{1} = 700\%$

28. (2) $3000 × 0.065 × $\frac{2}{3}$

6.5% = 0.065 and 8 months = $\frac{8}{12} = \frac{2}{3}$ year
$i = prt = \$3000 \times 0.065 \times \frac{2}{3}$

29. (4) $2 billion

13% = 0.13
0.13 × $15 billion =
$1.95 → $2 billion

30. (3) 50,000

492,385 → 500,000 and 10% = 0.1
0.1 × 500,000 = 50,000

Chapter 7

Basic Skills, page 62

1. 1 foot (ft)   = 12 inches (in.)
1 yard (yd)   = 36 inches
1 yard   = 3 feet
1 mile (mi)   = 5280 feet
1 mile   = 1760 yards

2. 1 pound (lb)   = 16 ounces (oz)
1 ton (T)   = 2000 pounds

3. 1 pint (pt)   = 16 ounces
1 cup   = 8 ounces
1 pint   = 2 cups
1 quart (qt)   = 2 pints
1 gallon (gal)   = 4 quarts

4. 1 minute (min) = 60 seconds (sec)
1 hour (hr)   = 60 minutes
1 day   = 24 hours
1 week (wk)   = 7 days
1 year (yr)   = 365 days

5. $\frac{1200}{2000} = \frac{3}{5}$ ton $\frac{6}{24} = \frac{1}{4}$ day

6. $\frac{6}{12} = \frac{1}{2}$ foot $\frac{12}{16} = \frac{3}{4}$ pound

7. $\frac{45}{60} = \frac{3}{4}$ hour $\frac{1}{4}$ gallon

8. $\frac{21}{36} = \frac{7}{12}$ yard $\frac{4}{12} = \frac{1}{3}$ foot

9. 2 × 16 = 32 ounces   6 × 12 = 72 inches

10. 3 × 60 = 180 seconds   5 × 3 = 15 feet

11. 10 × 2000 = 20,000 pounds   3 × 24 = 72 hours

12. 1 meter (m)   = 1000 millimeters (mm)
1 meter   = 100 centimeters (cm)
1 kilometer   = 1000 meters
1 decimeter (dm) = $\frac{1}{10}$ or 0.1 meter

13. 1 gram (g)   = 1000 milligrams (mg)
1 kilogram (kg)   = 1000 grams

14. 1 liter (L)   = 1000 milliliters (mL)
1 deciliter (dL)   = $\frac{1}{10}$ or 0.1 liter

15. 3.15 × 1000 = 3150 grams
2 × 1000 = 2000 meters

16. 4 × 100 = 400 centimeters
1.5 × 1000 = 1500 milliliters

17. 60 ÷ 100 = 0.6 meter
850 ÷ 1000 = 0.850 kilogram

18. 250 ÷ 1000 = 0.25 kilometer
135 ÷ 1000 = 0.135 liter

19. $\frac{20}{16}$ = 1.25 pounds

20. $\frac{21}{12} = 1\frac{9}{12} = 1\frac{3}{4}$ feet

21. $\frac{2500}{2000}$ = 1 ton 500 pounds

22. $\frac{90}{60}$ = 1.5 hours

23. $\frac{10}{4} = 2\frac{2}{4} = 2\frac{1}{2}$ gallons

24. $\frac{5680}{5280}$ = 1 mile 400 feet

25. A = $1\frac{1}{2}$ in.   B = $2\frac{3}{4}$ in.   C = 3 in.   D = $3\frac{5}{8}$ in.
E = $4\frac{1}{8}$ in.   F = $4\frac{3}{8}$ in.

26. G = 1 cm   H = 3.5 cm   I = 4.1 cm
J = 5.2 cm   K = 7.6 cm   L = 10.4 cm

GED Practice, Part I, page 65

1. $\frac{3}{16}$

2 lb = 2 × 16 = 32 oz

$\frac{6}{32} = \frac{3}{16}$

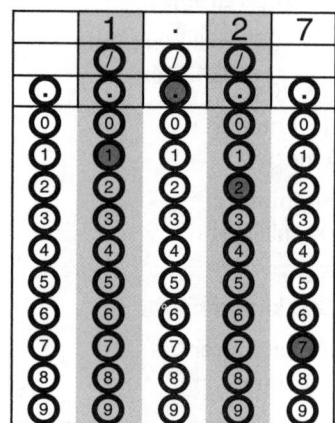

2. 1.27 kg

$\frac{0.6 + 1.41 + 1.8}{3} = \frac{3.81}{3} = 1.27$ kg

3. 4.9°

103.5° − 98.6° = 4.9°

4. (4) 37°

$C = \frac{5}{9}(F - 32)$

$C = \frac{5}{9}(98.6 - 32)$

$C = \frac{5}{9}(66.6)$

$C = 37$

5. (3) 7.5

reading is ≈ 75 volts

$\frac{1}{10} \times 75 = 7.5$

6. (3) $2.95

8 oz = $\frac{8}{16}$ = 0.5 lb

0.5 × $5.89 = $2.945 → $2.95

7. (5) 0.75

$\frac{32,670}{43,560} = 0.75$ acre

8. (2) 2.3

4.2 − 1.9 = 2.3 cm

9. (1) $6.46

1 lb 12 oz = $1\frac{12}{16}$ = 1.75 lb

1.75 × $3.69 = $6.4575 → $6.46

10. (1) 8

2 yd 9 in. = $2\frac{9}{36}$ = 2.25 yd

20 ÷ 2.25 = 8 + remainder

11. (5) 27 hr 2 min

$$\begin{array}{r} 7 \text{ hr} \quad 52 \text{ min} \\ 7 \text{ hr} \quad 16 \text{ min} \\ 10 \text{ hr} \quad 5 \text{ min} \\ +1 \text{ hr} \quad 49 \text{ min} \\ \hline 25 \text{ hr } 122 \text{ min} = 27 \text{ hr } 2 \text{ min} \end{array}$$

12. (2) $\dfrac{8}{9}$

$\dfrac{24}{27} = \dfrac{8}{9}$

13. (1) 144

2 hr 15 min $= 2\dfrac{15}{60} = 2.25$ hr

$d = rt = 64 \times 2.25 = 144$ miles

14. (4) 57.5

$0.453 \times 127 = 57.531 \rightarrow 57.5$ kg

15. (3) 32

$\dfrac{\text{miles}}{\text{minutes}} \qquad \dfrac{45}{60} = \dfrac{24}{x}$

$45x = 1440$

$x = 32$

16. (4) 5:43 P.M.

departure	= 8 :	55
regular travel time	= 7 hr	28 min
additional lateness	= 1 hr	20 min
total	= 16 hr 103 min = 17:43 =	
	5:43 P.M.	

GED Practice, Part II, page 67

17. 2.45

$\dfrac{245}{1000} = 2.45$

18. $\dfrac{5}{8}$

$\dfrac{10}{16} = \dfrac{5}{8}$

19. (4) 104°

$F = \dfrac{9}{5}C + 32$

$F = \dfrac{9}{5}(40) + 32$

$F = 72 + 32 = 104°$

20. (3) $\dfrac{11}{16}$

$$1\dfrac{5}{16} = \dfrac{5}{16} + \dfrac{16}{16} = \dfrac{21}{16}$$
$$-\dfrac{5}{8} = \qquad\qquad \dfrac{10}{16}$$
$$\rule{3cm}{0.4pt}$$
$$\dfrac{11}{16} \text{ in.}$$

21. (2) $\dfrac{3 \times 6}{16}$

$\dfrac{3 \text{ cans} \times 6 \text{ oz each}}{16 \text{ oz per pound}}$

22. (3) 35

crate 1 = 53 kg and crate 2 = 18 kg

$53 - 18 = 35$ kg

23. (4) $\dfrac{7}{8}$

$281 \rightarrow 280$ and $324 \rightarrow 320$

$\dfrac{280}{320} = \dfrac{7}{8}$

24. (2) 99.4°

25. (3) $\dfrac{55 \times 2 + 12 \times 1.5}{3.5}$

$d = rt + rt$

$d = 55 \times 2 + 12 \times 1.5$

average $= \dfrac{\text{distance}}{\text{total time}}$

average $= \dfrac{55 \times 2 + 12 \times 1.5}{.3.5}$

26. (3) 17

27. (4) $\dfrac{1}{2}$ quart

The other measurements are equal.

In fact, $\dfrac{7}{16}$ quart is shaded.

28. (2) 10%

before = 180 and after = 162

$180 - 162 = 18$

$\dfrac{18}{180} = \dfrac{1}{10} = 10\%$

29. (5) 16,753

1st dial	10,000
2nd dial	6,000
3rd dial	700
4th dial	50
5th dial	3
	16,753

Chapter 8

Basic Skills, page 70

1. D $75\% = \frac{3}{4}$ The remaining $\frac{1}{4}$ is divided equally.

2. A $\frac{1}{2}$ is for Bill. The remaining $\frac{1}{2}$ is divided equally between Steve and Tim.

3. C $\frac{3}{10} + \frac{2}{10} = \frac{5}{10} = \frac{1}{2}$
   $\frac{1}{2}$ is divided into 30% and 20%. The remaining $\frac{1}{2}$ is for all other expenses.

4. B The three parts are the same.

5. (3) percent   7. 2%

6. (2) years   8. 2000

9. (3) The percentage of air travel reservations made online has increased steadily.

10. 17
    in order: 12 14 14 <u>17</u> 22 23 24

11. 18
    $\frac{12 + 14 + 14 + 17 + 22 + 23 + 24}{7} = \frac{126}{7} = 18$

12. 14
    The only age that occurs more than once is 14.

13. 4 A.M.   16. $55° - 40° = 15°$

14. 35°   17. (3) noon to 4 P.M.

15. 65°

18. C The graph falls from left to right.

19. D The graph rises more and more sharply from left to right.

20. A The graph remains constant (horizontal).

21. E The graph falls more and more sharply from left to right.

22. B The graph rises steadily from left to right.

23. $768 - $659 = $109

24. $7540
    $52 \times \$618 - 52 \times \$473 =$
    $\$32,136 - \$24,596 = \$7,540$

25. 28%
    $\frac{\text{difference}}{\text{men's median}}$ $\frac{\$791 - \$618}{\$618} \times 100\% = \frac{\$173}{\$618} \times 100\%$
    $= 27.99\% \rightarrow 28\%$

26. $\frac{1}{3}$
    total = 7 + 8 + 4 + 5 = 24
    $\frac{\text{favorable outcomes}}{\text{possible outcomes}} = \frac{8}{24} = \frac{1}{3}$

27. $\frac{2}{11}$
    total = 24 − 2 = 22
    $\frac{\text{favorable}}{\text{possible}} = \frac{4}{22} = \frac{2}{11}$

GED Practice, Part I, page 74

1. 35.3

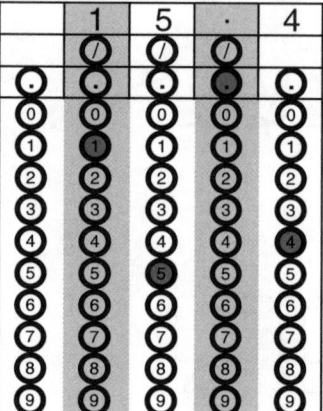

2. 15.4
   $41.0 - 25.6 = 15.4$

3. 24.2

$$\frac{\text{change}}{\text{original}} = \frac{41 - 33}{33} = \frac{8}{33} \approx 0.2424 \rightarrow 24.2\%$$

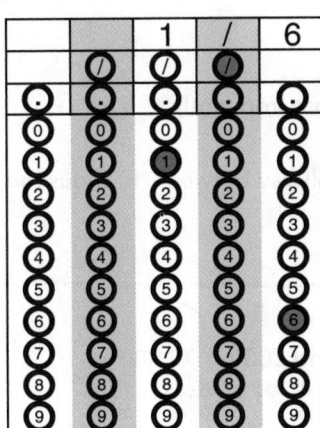

4. (2) $66\frac{2}{3}\%$

$$\frac{18\%}{27\%} = \frac{2}{3} = 66\frac{2}{3}\%$$

5. (1) 46%

27% + 18% + 9% = 54%

100% − 54% = 46%

6. (4) 97.2°

27% = 0.27

0.27 × 360° = 97.2°

7. (3) 10

6 + 4 = 10

8. (2) 28%

total = 4 + 6 + 8 + 5 + 2 = 25

younger than 30 = 5 + 2 = 7

$$\frac{7}{25} = 0.28 = 28\%$$

9. (3) 30 − 39

10. (2) $\frac{13}{21}$

total = 4 + 26 + 12 = 42

$$\frac{\text{favorable}}{\text{possible}} = \frac{26}{42} = \frac{13}{21}$$

11. (1) $\frac{1}{10}$

total = 42 − 2 = 40

$$\frac{\text{favorable}}{\text{possible}} = \frac{4}{40} = \frac{1}{10}$$

12. (2) $320

0.04 × $8,000 = $320

13. (4) $525

$12,800 − $11,000 = $1,800

0.045 × $1,800 = $81

$444 + $81 = $525

14. (3) $1197

$25,000 − $17,000 = $8,000

0.059 × $8,000 = $472

$725 + $472 = $1197

15. (1) $\frac{3}{8}$

total tiles = 6 + 10 = 16

$$\frac{\text{favorable}}{\text{possible}} = \frac{6}{16} = \frac{3}{8}$$

GED Practice, Part II, page 77

16. (4) 3:5

13 + 15 + 9 + 8 = 45 men

17 + 21 + 17 + 20 = 75 women

men:women = 45:75 = 3:5

17. (2) 25%

math students = 13 + 17 = 30

$$\frac{30}{120} = \frac{1}{4} = 25\%$$

18. $\frac{1}{6}$

total students = 13 + 17 + 15 + 21 + 9 + 17 + 8 + 20 = 120

$$\frac{\text{favorable}}{\text{possible}} = \frac{20}{120} = \frac{1}{6}$$

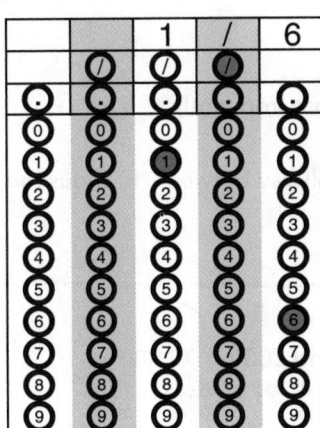

19. $\frac{1}{8}$

$$\frac{\text{favorable}}{\text{possible}} = \frac{15}{120} = \frac{1}{8}$$

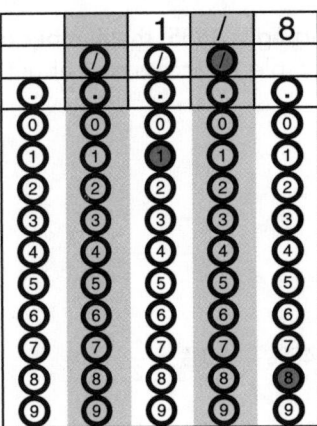

20. (2) 20

cheetah − lion = 70 − 50 = 20 mph

21. (4) twice

$$\frac{\text{lion}}{\text{elephant}} = \frac{50}{25} = \frac{2}{1}$$

22. (2) 10

$$15 \text{ min} = \frac{15}{60} = \frac{1}{4} \text{ hr}$$

$$d = rt = 40 \times \frac{1}{4} = 10 \text{ miles}$$

23. (4) 4–5

$$\frac{\text{miles}}{\text{minutes}} = \frac{70}{60} = \frac{5}{x}$$

$$70x = 300$$

$$x = 4.28 \text{ or } 4\text{–}5 \text{ minutes}$$

24. (3) 5.5

$$\text{total} = 10 + 4 + 1 + 7 + 2 + 5 +$$

$$8 + 7 + 4 + 7 = 55$$

$$\frac{55}{10} = 5.5$$

25. (3) 6

in order: 1 2 4 4 <u>5</u> <u>7</u> 7 7 8 10

$$\frac{5 + 7}{2} = \frac{12}{2} = 6$$

26. (4) 7

7 was chosen most frequently.

27. (1) 15,000

The line stops halfway between 10 thousand and 20 thousand.

28. (3) 1990

29. (5) $\frac{30,000}{40,000}$

1985 = 40,000 and 2000 = 70,000

$$\frac{\text{change}}{\text{original}} = \frac{70,000 - 40,000}{40,000} = \frac{30,000}{40,000}$$

30. (2) 1980–1985

The graph rises most sharply for these 5 years.

31. (4) The number of users will increase by about 10,000.

Every 5 years starting in 1985, the number of households with cable TV access rose about 10,000.

32. (3) twice

a year = 24%

a week or two = 12%

$$\frac{24\%}{12\%} = \frac{2}{1}$$

33. (2) $\frac{1}{2}$

a few months = 48% → 50% = $\frac{1}{2}$

34. (3) 180

indefinitely = 15% and 1198 → 1200

$0.015 \times 1200 = 180$

35. (3) 80

men + women = 15 + 65 = 80

36. (4) The number of men increased by about 10. The bars for men rise from about 15 to about 25.

37. (2) 45

The bar stops halfway between 40 and 50.

38. (5) The number of teachers will remain about the same, but there will be more men than women.

The trend is that the number of men increases while the number of women decreases, but the total remains about 80.

39. (4) 20 pounds − $1\frac{1}{2}$ hours

The person who lost 20 pounds jogged an average of only $1\frac{1}{2}$ hours per week. This point is farthest off the generally rising line corresponding to weight loss and hours of jogging.

40. (2) More jogging results in greater weight loss.

Generally, the greater the weight loss, the more hours the participants spent jogging.

Chapter 9

Basic Skills, page 82

1. vertical

2. horizontal

3. parallel and horizontal

4. perpendicular

5. right

6. reflex

7. acute

8. obtuse

9. acute

10. obtuse

11. straight

12. right

13. supplementary or adjacent

∠b = 180° − 62° = 118°

14. complementary or adjacent

∠b = 90° − 49° = 41°

15. vertical

∠b = 75° because vertical angles are equal.

16. adjacent or supplementary

∠b = 180° − 58° = 122° because these adjacent angles are supplementary.

17. rectangle

18. square

19. triangle

20. parallelogram

21. trapezoid

22. rectangle

23. trapezoid

24. triangle

25. perimeter

26. volume

27. area

28. $P = 2l + 2w$
$P = 2(15) + 2(8) = 30 + 16 = 46$ in.

$P = 4s$
$P = 4(6) = 24$ ft

$P = s_1 + s_2 + s_3$
$P = 9 + 12 + 15 = 36$ yd

29. $A = lw$
$A = (15)(8) = 120$ sq in.

$A = s^2$
$A = 6^2$
$A = (6)(6) = 36$ sq ft

$A = \frac{1}{2}bh$
$A = \frac{1}{2}(12)(9) = 54$ sq yd

30. circumference
31. diameter
32. radius
33. π (pi)
34. 360°

35. $r = \frac{d}{2} = \frac{40}{2} = 20$ in.

36. $C = \pi d$
$C = 3.14(40) = 125.6$ in.

37. $A = \pi r^2$
$A = 3.14(20)^2 = 3.14(400) = 1256$ sq in.

38. rectangular solid
39. cube
40. cone
41. rectangular solid
42. cylinder
43. square pyramid

44. $V = lwh$
$V = (8)(5)(4) = 160$ cu in.

45. $V = s^3$
$V = 3^3 = 3 \times 3 \times 3 = 27$ cu ft

46. isosceles
47. right
48. isosceles
49. equilateral
50. scalene
51. right

52. $\angle B = 180° - 45° - 77° = 58°$

53. Side AB is longest because it is opposite the largest angle, $\angle C$.

54. Side BC is shortest because it is opposite the smallest angle, $\angle A$.

55. Yes

The ratio of the length to the width for both triangles is 4:3.

$8:6 = 4:3$ and $12:9 = 4:3$

56. No

Although the angles are the same, the corresponding sides are not equal.

57. (3) $5^2 + 8^2 = c^2$

The Pythagorean relationship states that, for a right triangle, the sum of the squares of the legs, 5 and 8, equals the square of the hypotenuse, c.

GED Practice, Part I, page 87

1. $180° - 71.5° = 108.5°$

2. $A = s^2 = (\frac{5}{8})^2 = \frac{5}{8} \times \frac{5}{8} = \frac{25}{64}$ sq in.

3. $P = 3s = 3(1.35) = 4.05$ m

4. (3) 37

$P = 2l + 2w$

$P = 2(10\frac{1}{2}) + 2(8)$

$P = 21 + 16$

$P = 37$ in.

5. (2) 84

$A = lw$

$A = 10.5 \times 8$

$A = 84$ sq in.

6. (4) 16.8

$P = s_1 + s_2 + s_3$

$P = 4.2 + 5.6 + 7$

$P = 16.8$ m

7. (1) 11.8

$A = \frac{1}{2}bh$

$A = 0.5 \times 5.6 \times 4.2$

$A = 11.76 \to 11.8$ m^2

8. (3) 94

$C = \pi d$

$C = 3.14 \times 30$

$C = 94.2 \to 94$ in.

9. (4) 707

$r = \frac{d}{2} = \frac{30}{2} = 15$ in.

$A = \pi r^2$

$A = 3.14(15)^2$

$A = 3.14(225)$

$A = 706.5 \to 707$ sq in.

10. (4) 324

$A = \frac{1}{2}(b_1 + b_2)h$

$A = \frac{1}{2}(24 + 30) \times 12$

$A = 6(54)$

$A = 324$ sq ft

11. (2) 36°

$180° - 72° - 72° = 36°$

12. (3) 2.0

$P = 4s$

$P = 4(0.5)$

$P = 2.0$ m

13. (3) 216

$V = lwh$

$V = 12 \times 12 \times 1.5$

$V = 216$ cu in.

14. (4) $\frac{1}{1728}$

$V = s^3$

$V = (12)^3$

$V = 12 \times 12 \times 12$

$V = 1728$ cu in.

$\frac{1 \text{ cu in.}}{1 \text{ cu ft}} = \frac{1}{1728}$

15. (1) 262

$V = \frac{1}{3}\pi r^2 h$

$V = \frac{1}{3}(3.14)(5)^2(10)$

$V = 261.6 \to 262$ cu in.

16. (1) 20

$a^2 + b^2 = c^2$

$a^2 + 48^2 = 52^2$

$a^2 + 2304 = 2704$

$a^2 = 400$

$a = \sqrt{400}$

$a = 20$ miles

17. (5) 22,500

$V = lwh$

$V = 30 \times 20 \times 5$

$V = 3000$ cu ft

$7.5 \times 3000 = 22,500$ gallons

18. (4) 80

$P = 2l + 2w$

$P = 2(18) + 2(12)$

$P = 36 + 24$

$P = 60$

9 in. $= \frac{9}{12} = 0.75$ foot

$60 \div 0.75 = 80$ bricks

19. (4) 47

$A = lw + lw$

$A = 20(15) + 10(12)$

$A = 300 + 120$

$A = 420$ sq ft

1 sq yd $= 3 \times 3 = 9$ sq ft

$420 \div 9 = 46.6 \to 47$ sq yd

20. (2) 20

base of large triangle $= 3 + 9 = 12$ ft

$\frac{\text{short side}}{\text{long side}} = \frac{3}{5} = \frac{12}{x}$

$3x = 60$

$x = 20$ ft

GED Practice, Part II, page 90

21. $90° - 28.5° = 61.5°$

22. $A = s^2$

$A = (1.6)^2$

$A = 1.6 \times 1.6 = 2.56$ m²

23. (4) $(40)(20) + (0.5)(40)(15)$

The area is a rectangle + a triangle.

Area of rectangle = $(40)(20)$.

The height of the triangle is $35 - 20 = 15$ ft.

Area of triangle is $(0.5)(40)(15)$.

24. (3) $\dfrac{C}{d}$

For any circle, π is the ratio of the circumference to the diameter.

25. (1) $AC = DF$

This satisfies the *side angle side* requirement for congruence.

26. (5) 24π

$d = 2r = 2(12) = 24$

$C = \pi d$

$C = \pi(24) = 24\pi$

27. (5) AB

The height AB is perpendicular to an extension of the base CD.

28. (4) $132°$

$\angle ADB = 180° - 90° - 42° = 48°$

$\angle BDC = 180° - 48° = 132°$

29. (2) 162

Area of table = $lw = 6 \times 3 = 18$ sq ft

4 in. $= \dfrac{4}{12} = \dfrac{1}{3}$ foot

Area of 1 tile $= \dfrac{1}{3} \times \dfrac{1}{3} = \dfrac{1}{9}$ sq ft

$18 \div \dfrac{1}{9} = 18 \times 9 = 162$ tiles

Or

1 sq ft $= 12 \times 12 = 144$ sq in.

and 1 tile $= 4 \times 4 = 16$ sq in.

$144 \div 16 = 9$ tiles per square foot

$9 \times 18 = 162$ tiles

30. (4) $\dfrac{180° - 55°}{2}$

$180° - 55° = $ sum of the two base angles

$\dfrac{180° - 55°}{2} = $ each base angle

31. (4) 240

6 in. $= \dfrac{6}{12} = \dfrac{1}{2}$ foot

$V = lwh$

$V = 24 \times 20 \times \dfrac{1}{2}$

$V = 240$ cu ft

32. (5) $\angle d, \angle e, \angle h$

These are the three other acute angles besides $\angle a$.

33. (1) $360°$

The four angles form a complete circle.

34. (1) $(30)(15) + (15)(10)$

The larger part of the deck is 30×15. The smaller part is 15×10.

35. (3) 50%

The base of the triangle is the length of the rectangle, and the height of the triangle is the width of the rectangle. The area of the triangle is $\dfrac{1}{2} bh$ and the area of the rectangle is bh. In other words, the area of the triangle is $\dfrac{1}{2}$ or 50% of the area of the rectangle.

36. (2) 1–2 miles

In one revolution, the wheels travel $C = \pi d = 3.14(2) = 6.28$ feet.

In 1000 revolutions, the wheels travel $1000(6.28) = 6280$ feet.

One mile = 5280 feet. Therefore, the wheels travel between 1 and 2 miles.

37. (2) 100

$$\frac{\text{short}}{\text{long}} = \frac{12}{40} = \frac{30}{x}$$

$$12x = 1200$$

$$x = 100 \text{ feet}$$

38. (4) $4r^2 - \pi r^2$

The area of one small square is r^2, and the area of the large square is $4r^2$.

The area of the circle is πr^2.

The shaded part is the area of the large square minus the area of the circle, or $4r^2 - \pi r^2$.

39. (3) $12\frac{1}{2}\%$

The area of the house is $lw = (40)(25) = 1000$ sq ft.

The area of the lot is $lw = (100)(80) = 8000$ sq ft.

$$\frac{\text{area of house}}{\text{area of lot}} = \frac{1000}{8000} = \frac{1}{8} = 12\frac{1}{2}\%$$

40. (5) 64

The radius of the small cylinder is $\frac{6}{12} = 0.5$ ft.

$$\frac{\text{volume of large container}}{\text{volume of small container}} = \frac{\pi r^2 h}{\pi r^2 h} = \frac{3.14 \times 2^2 \times 4}{3.14 \times (0.5)^2 \times 1} =$$

$$\frac{4 \times 4}{0.25} = \frac{16}{0.25} = 64$$

Chapter 10

Basic Skills, page 94

1. $8 > 0$ $+4 > -6$ $-7 < -3$

2. $\frac{3}{3} = 1$ $-10 < 0$ $-\frac{15}{3} = -5$

3. $-6 > -9$ $\frac{18}{2} = \frac{36}{4}$ $-7 < 2$

4. $+8 - 14 = -6$ $-2 - 11 = -13$

   $-3 + 8 = +5$

5. $(-7) + (-3) = -10$ $-10 + 16 = +6$

   $(+4) + (-4) = 0$

6. $(-3) - (-4) = -3 + 4 = +1$

   $(-7) - (+8) = -7 - 8 = -15$

   $12 - (-3) = 12 + 3 = 15$

7. $(-4)(+8) = -32$ $(-9)(-9) = +81$

   $(+7)(-10) = -70$

8. $-\frac{1}{3} \cdot 48 = -16$ $-\frac{2}{3} \cdot -\frac{1}{2} = \frac{1}{3}$

   $-5 \cdot 0 = 0$

9. $\frac{-20}{-10} = 2$ $-\frac{18}{24} = -\frac{3}{4}$ $-\frac{72}{8} = -9$

10. $7(4 - 9) = 7(-5) = -35$

   $3(-4) + 7 = -12 + 7 = -5$

   $\frac{8 - 20}{3} = \frac{-12}{3} = -4$

11. $a + 7 = 20$ $8b = 32$ $\frac{c}{3} = 15$

   $a = 13$ $b = 4$ $c = 45$

12. $d - 6 = 12$ $12e = 9$ $5 = 2f$

   $d = 18$ $e = \frac{3}{4}$ $2\frac{1}{2} = f$

13. $4g - 3 = 25$ $2h + 9 = 10$ $2 = 5m - 3$

   $4g = 28$ $2h = 1$ $5 = 5m$

   $g = 7$ $h = \frac{1}{2}$ $1 = m$

14. $7n - 2n + 4 = 19$ $6p = p + 10$ $9a - 4 = 3a + 20$

   $5n + 4 = 19$ $5p = 10$ $6a - 4 = 20$

   $5n = 15$ $p = 2$ $6a = 24$

   $n = 3$ $a = 4$

15. $3(y - 5) = 6$ $8x - 3 < 13$ $2s - 7 \geq 9$

   $3y - 15 = 6$ $8x < 16$ $2s \geq 16$

   $3y = 21$ $x < 2$ $s \geq 8$

   $y = 7$

16. $x - 11$

17. $4x$

18. $\frac{x}{5}$

19. $\frac{8}{x}$

20. $30 - x$

21. $x + 9$ or $9 + x$

22. $\frac{1}{2}x$ or $\frac{x}{2}$

23. $2x - 10$

24. $x + 8 = 23$

   $x = 15$

25. $5x - 6 = 29$

   $5x = 35$

   $x = 7$

26. $\frac{1}{2}x + 3 = 10$

   $\frac{1}{2}x = 7$

   $x = 14$

27. $2x - 9 = x + 4$

   $x = 13$

28. $a + 10$

29. $\frac{3}{4}c$ or $0.75c$

30. $0.25t$ or $\frac{1}{4}t$ or $\frac{t}{4}$

31. $\frac{w}{5}$

32. $p - 20$

33. $s - 0.15s$ or $0.85s$

34. $b + 0.06b$ or $1.06b$

35. $w + 6$

GED Practice, Part I, page 97

1. 856

$10^3 - 12^2 =$

$10 \times 10 \times 10 - 12 \times 12 =$

$1000 - 144 = 856$

2. 1.4

$c + 3.8 = 5.2$

$c = 1.4$

3. $\frac{5}{8}$

$8x - 3 = 2$

$8x = 5$

$x = \frac{5}{8}$

4. (2) 8

$14 - 9 + 3 = 17 - 9 = 8$

5. (2) $5m - 4$

$7m - 12 - 2m + 8 = 5m - 4$

6. (5) -16

$2(-3) - 10 = -6 - 10 = -16$

7. (3) 19

$(23) + (-9) - (-5) =$

$23 - 9 + 5 = 28 - 9 = 19$

8. (2) $a = -4$

$6(\frac{1}{2}) - 7 = 3 - 7 = -4$

9. (4) $s = \frac{1}{2}$

$6s - 1 = 2s + 1$

$4s = 2$

$s = \frac{2}{4} = \frac{1}{2}$

10. (1) 10

$5(y - 4) = 2(y + 5)$

$5y - 20 = 2y + 10$

$3y = 30$

$y = 10$

11. (2) 16

$A = \frac{1}{2}bh$

$128 = \frac{1}{2}(16)h$

$128 = 8h$

$16 = h$

12. (4) 36

$lw = s^2$

$25l = 30^2$

$25l = 900$

$l = 36$

13. (1) $l = \frac{s^2}{w}$

$lw = s^2$

$l = \frac{s^2}{w}$

14. (4) $-1\frac{9}{16}$

The other values all equal -1.75.

The value could be $-1\frac{12}{16}$.

15. (5) $14x + 4$

$P = 2l + 2w$

$P = 2(4x + 2) + 2(3x)$

$P = 8x + 4 + 6x$

$P = 14x + 4$

16. (3) 74

$P = 14x + 4$

$P = 14(5) + 4 = 70 + 4 = 74$

17. (1) $8x - 7 = 5x + 20$

"Decreased by" means to subtract.

"Increased by" means to add.

18. (3) 9

$8x - 7 = 5x + 20$

$3x = 27$

$x = 9$

19. (4) 84

x = games lost, and $x + 6$ = games won

$$x + x + 6 = 162$$
$$2x + 6 = 162$$
$$2x = 156$$
$$x = 78$$
$$x + 6 = 78 + 6 = 84$$

20. (2) $482

Karen makes x.

Steve makes $x + 42$.

Joe makes $x - 150$.

$$x + x + 42 + x - 150 = 1212$$
$$3x - 108 = 1212$$
$$3x = 1320$$
$$x = 440$$
$$x + 42 = 440 + 42 = 482$$

GED Practice, Part II, page 99

21. $\frac{3}{5}$

$$\frac{3^2}{21 - 6} = \frac{9}{15} = \frac{3}{5}$$

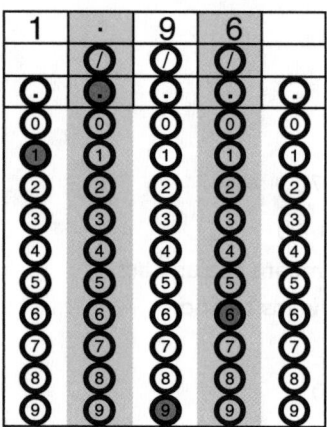

22. 1.96

$$(-1.4)^2 = (-1.4)(-1.4) = 1.96$$

23. (1) $5x + 1$

$$x + 2 + x - 1 + 3x = 5x + 1$$

24. (2) 36

$$5(7) + 1 = 35 + 1 = 36$$

25. (5) 72°

$$4x + 3x + 3x = 180$$
$$10x = 180$$
$$x = 18$$
$$4(18) = 72$$

26. (5) 4

$$5n - 4 \leq 11$$
$$5n \leq 15$$
$$n \leq 3$$

Since n must be less than or equal to 3, 4 is not an answer.

27. (3) $2w + 3$

twice = $2w$

$3 more = $2w + 3$

28. (3) $7.50

$$2w + 3 = 18$$
$$2w = 15$$
$$w = 7.50$$

29. (1) $y = x^2$

In each case, y is the square of x.

30. (4) $t = \frac{d}{60}$

Substitute 60 mph for r in $d = rt$.

Then solve for t.

$$d = 60t$$
$$\frac{d}{60} = t$$

31. (4) $\frac{4}{3}$

The inverse of $\frac{3}{4}$ is $\frac{4}{3}$.

$$\frac{3}{4}x \cdot \frac{4}{3} = x$$

32. (5) $l = \frac{P - 2w}{2}$

Solve for l in $P = 2l + 2w$.

33. (2) $1.1m$

Remember that $m = 1m$.

$$m + 0.1m = 1.1m$$

34. (3) $0.8p$

$$20\% = 0.2$$
$$p - 0.2p = 0.8p$$

35. (2) $b = 2a + 1$

Each number in b is 1 more than twice the value in a.

36. (3) $c = 1.06nr$

$$6\% = 0.06$$
$$c = nr + 0.06nr = 1.06nr$$

37. (5) $h = \dfrac{V}{lw}$

Solve $V = lwh$ for h.

Divide both sides by lw.

$\dfrac{V}{lw} = h$

38. (3) 56°

$2x + 3x + 5 = 90$

$5x + 5 = 90$

$5x = 85$

$x = 17$

$3(17) + 5 = 51 + 5 = 56$

39. (2) 32

$w = x$

$l = x + 6$

$P = 2l + 2w = 116$

$2(x + 6) + 2x = 116$

$2x + 12 + 2x = 116$

$4x + 12 = 116$

$4x = 104$

$x = 26$

$26 + 6 = 32$

40. (5) $V = w^3$

$l = 2w$ and $h = \dfrac{w}{2}$

$V = lwh$

$V = (2w)(w)(\dfrac{w}{2})$

$V = w^3$

Chapter 11

Basic Skills, page 103

1. Point $A = (6, 5)$

Point $B = (0, 4)$

Point $C = (-5, 4)$

Point $D = (-6, 0)$

Point $E = (-2, -3)$

Point $F = (3, -7)$

2. Point D

3. Point A

4. Point B

5.

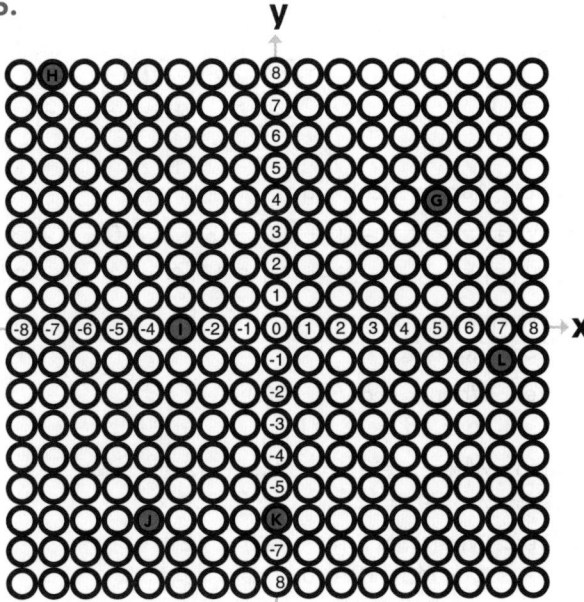

6. Point I

7. Point J

8. Point K

9. 6 units

10. 28 units

The distance from A to D is 8.

$P = 2l + 2w$

$P = 2(8) + 2(6) = 16 + 12 = 28$

11. 48 square units

$A = lw$

$A = (8)(6) = 48$

12. 10 units

$\text{distance} = \sqrt{(x_2 - x_1)^2 + (y_2 - y_1)^2}$

$= \sqrt{(11 - 3)^2 + (8 - 2)^2}$

$= \sqrt{(8)^2 + (6)^2}$

$= \sqrt{64 + 36}$

$= \sqrt{100}$

$= 10$

13. $\dfrac{6}{8} = \dfrac{3}{4}$ (This is also the slope of the diagonal line from A to C.)

14. graph C

15. graph D

16. graph B

17. graph A

18. When $x = 3$, $y = 2(3) + 5 = 6 + 5 = 11$.

19. When $x = -4$, $y = 2(-4) + 5 = -8 + 5 = -3$.

20. When $x = 0$, $y = 2(0) + 5 = 0 + 5 = 5$.

21. (0, 5) When $x = 0$, the value of y is 5.

22. $\text{slope} = \dfrac{y_2 - y_1}{x_2 - x_1} = \dfrac{8 - 2}{7 - 1} = \dfrac{6}{6} = 1$

23. $48 = 2 \times 2 \times 2 \times 2 \times 3$

24. $\sqrt{75} = \sqrt{25 \cdot 3} = 5\sqrt{3}$

25. $\sqrt{98} = \sqrt{49 \cdot 2} = 7\sqrt{2}$

26. $x \cdot x = x^2$

27. $4m^4 \cdot 3m = 12m^5$

28. $\frac{c}{c} = 1$

29. $\frac{a^5}{a^2} = a^3$

30. $\frac{12n^3}{6n^2} = 2n$

31. $6x - 4 = 2(3x - 2)$

32. $8c + 10cd = 2c(4 + 5d)$

33. When $x = 0$, $y = 0^2 + 4(0) + 3 = 0 + 0 + 3 = 3$.

34. When $x = 3$, $y = 3^2 + 4(3) + 3 = 9 + 12 + 3 = 24$.

35. When $x = -5$, $y = (-5)^2 + 4(-5) + 3 =$
$25 - 20 + 3 = 8$.

36. Yes. When $x = 6$, $6^2 - 8(6) + 12 =$
$36 - 48 + 12 = 0$.

37. No. When $x = 3$, $3^2 - 8(3) + 12 =$
$9 - 24 + 12 = -3 \neq 0$.

38. Yes. When $x = 2$, $2^2 - 8(2) + 12 =$
$4 - 16 + 12 = 0$.

GED Practice, Part I, page 107

1. $(4, -6)$ is 4 units to the right of the vertical axis and 6 units below the horizontal axis.

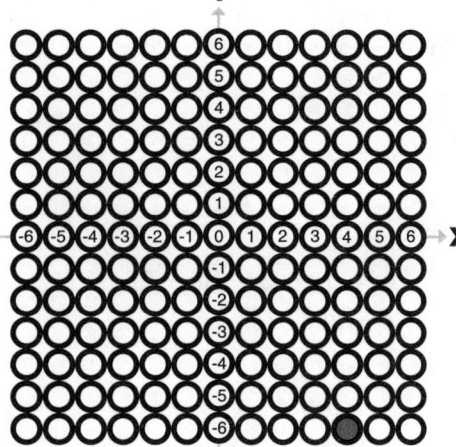

2. $(-3, -5)$ is 3 units to the left of the vertical axis and 5 units below the horizontal axis.

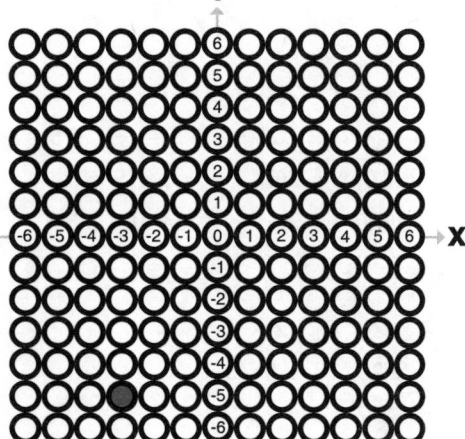

3. $(-2, 4)$ is 2 units to the left of the vertical axis and 4 units above the horizontal axis.

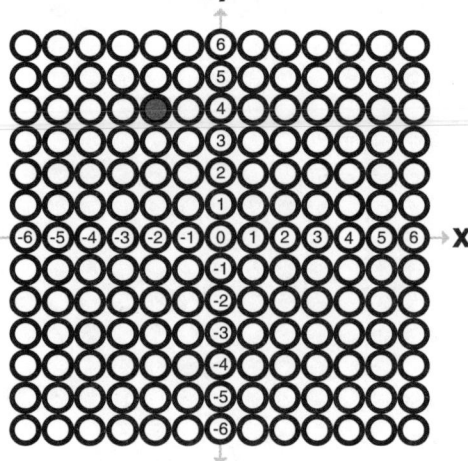

4. (4) $(-8, 15)$

The point is 8 units to the left of the y-axis and 15 units above the x-axis.

5. (1) $(12, -3)$

The point is 12 units to the right of the y-axis and 3 units below the x-axis.

6. (2) 12

Point A is 3 units to the left of the y-axis and point B is 9 units to the right.

The distance between the points is $3 + 9 = 12$.

7. (5) 56

The length is $6 + 10 = 16$, and the width is $22 - 10 = 12$.

$P = 2l + 2w = 2(16) + 2(12) = 32 + 24 = 56$

8. (4) 192

$A = lw = (16)(12) = 192$ square units

9. (3) 20

$$\text{distance} = \sqrt{(x_2 - x_1)^2 + (y_2 - y_1)^2}$$
$$= \sqrt{(10 - (-6))^2 + (22 - 10)^2}$$
$$= \sqrt{(16)^2 + (12)^2}$$
$$= \sqrt{256 + 144}$$
$$= \sqrt{400}$$
$$= 20 \text{ units}$$

10. (3) 132

$y = 12^2 - 12 = 144 - 12 = 132$

11. (5) 26

$y = (-3)^2 - 5(-3) + 2 = 9 + 15 + 2 = 26$

12. (2) $12a^3b^4$

Multiply 3 by 4: $3(4) = 12$.

Add the exponents of a: $1 + 2 = 3$.

Add the exponents of b: $1 + 3 = 4$.

13. (3) $6x^2$

$A = \frac{1}{2}bh = \frac{1}{2}(4x)(3x) = 6x^2$

14. (5) $7n^2 - 35n$

$7n(n) = 7n^2$ and $7n(5) = 35n$

15. (4) $\frac{5}{9}$

slope $= \frac{y_2 - y_1}{x_2 - x_1} = \frac{9 - 4}{12 - 3} = \frac{5}{9}$

16. (1) $5\sqrt{7}$

$\sqrt{175} = \sqrt{25 \cdot 7} = 5\sqrt{7}$

17. (3) 73

$\frac{\text{opposite}}{\text{adjacent}} = 1.732$

$\frac{x}{42} = 1.732$

$x = 72.744 \rightarrow 73$ ft

18. (4) $x = 5$ and $x = -6$

When $x = 5$, $y = (5)^2 + 5 - 30 = 25 + 5 - 30 = 0$.

When $x = -6$, $y = (-6)^2 + (-6) - 30 = 36 - 6 - 30 = 0$.

GED Practice, Part II, page 109

19. (0, 4)

When $x = 0$, $y = 5(0) + 4 = 4$.

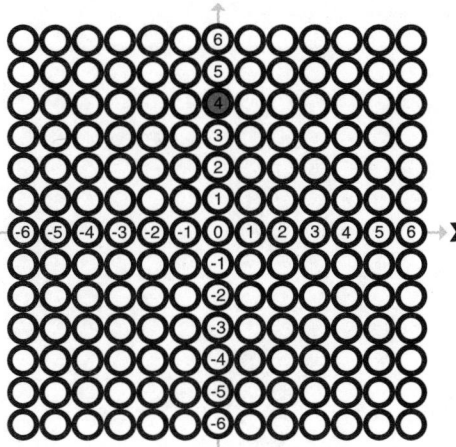

20. (5, 5)

The point is 4 units to the right of (1, 5) and 3 units above (5, 2).

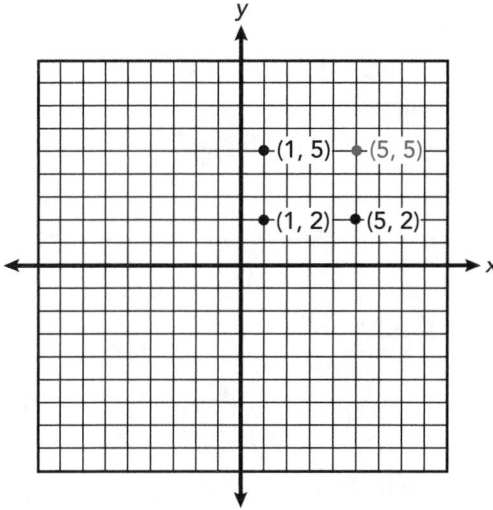

21. (−4, −3)

The point is 4 units left of the y-axis and 3 units below the x-axis.

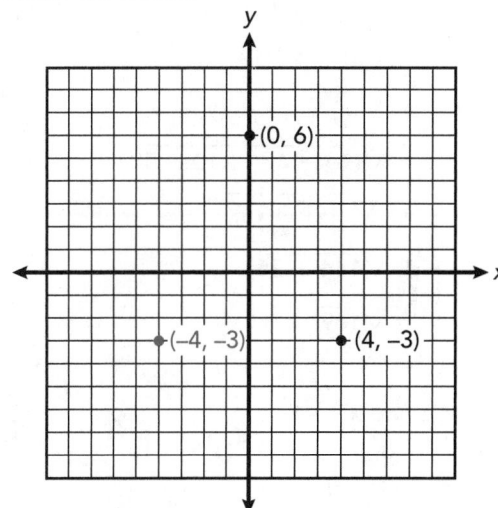

22. (4) $y = x - 2$

This is the only equation in the list that, when you substitute 0 for x, results in a negative value of y.

23. (5) $4\sqrt{2}$

distance $= \sqrt{(4)^2 + (4)^2}$

$= \sqrt{16 + 16}$

$= \sqrt{32}$

$= \sqrt{16 \cdot 2}$

$= 4\sqrt{2}$

24. (3) 14

$y = (-4)^2 - (-4) - 6 = 16 + 4 - 6 = 14$

25. (4) $2 \times 5 \times 5$

Although the other products result in 50, only choice (4) uses prime numbers.

26. (4) $12a^2 + 15a$

$A = lw = (4a + 5)(3a) = 12a^2 + 15a$

27. (2) $(0, -8)$

When $x = 0$, $y = \frac{0}{2} - 8 = -8$.

28. (5) $18m^2 - 9m$

$9m(2m - 1) = 18m^2 - 9m$

29. (2) -1

$\text{slope} = \frac{y_2 - y_1}{x_2 - x_1}$

$\text{slope} = \frac{7 - (-5)}{-5 - 7} = \frac{7 + 5}{-12} = \frac{12}{-12} = -1$

30. (1) $3m^2 n^3$

Divide 15 by 5: $\frac{15}{5} = 3$.

Subtract the powers of m: $3 - 1 = 2$.

Subtract the powers of n: $4 - 1 = 3$.

31. (3) $x = 7$

When $x = 7$, $7^2 - 3(7) - 28 = 49 - 21 - 28 = 0$.

32. (3) 13

$\begin{aligned}
\text{distance} &= \sqrt{(x_2 - x_1)^2 + (y_2 - y_1)^2} \\
&= \sqrt{(16 - 4)^2 + (10 - 5)^2} \\
&= \sqrt{(12)^2 + (5)^2} \\
&= \sqrt{144 + 25} \\
&= \sqrt{169} \\
&= 13
\end{aligned}$

33. (1) $x = 3$ and $x = -8$

When $x = 3$, $y = (3)^2 + 5(3) - 24 = 9 + 15 - 24 = 0$.

When $x = -8$, $y = (-8)^2 + 5(-8) - 24 = 64 - 40 - 24 = 0$.

34. (4) $\frac{80 - 70}{3 - 1}$

Choice (4) does not use corresponding points. The x values for $80 - 70$ are $3 - 2$.

35. (1) 10

You can use answer choices (1), (2), (3), or (5) in the last problem to calculate the slope. For example, for answer choice (1), $\frac{90 - 80}{4 - 3} = \frac{10}{1} = 10$.